# BATHROOM BOOK
## of
# ONTARIO
# TRIVIA
### Weird, Wacky and Wild

## René Josef Biberstein

BLUE
BIKE
BOOKS

The Publisher Blue Bike Books

**Library and Archives Canada Cataloguing in Publication**

Biberstein, Rene Josef, 1981–
   Bathroom book of Ontario trivia / Rene Josef Biberstein.

(Bathroom books of Canada ; 6)
ISBN-13: 978-1-897278-03-1
ISBN-10: 1-897278-03-9

   1. Ontario—Miscellanea. I. Title. II. Series.

FC3061.B53 2006          971.3          C2006-902987-3

*Project Director:* Nicholle Carrière
*Project Editor:* Timothy le Riche
*Illustrations:* Roger Garcia
*Cover Image:* Roger Garcia

*PC: P5*

# DEDICATION

To Gordon Gray, my grandfather, who knows more about
Ontario and most other things than I ever will.

# ACKNOWLEDGEMENTS

Thanks to Laurel Christie for her help with natural history.
And, for being supportive and for not laughing at me too much.
Thanks also to black coffee, for its unique ability to maximize
human potential.

# CONTENTS

# INTRODUCTION

When I was about 10 years old, I started reading the newspaper nearly every day. Around the same time, my parents began buying me little booklets from the supermarket checkout area, with glossy covers and newsprint pages, and with names such as *Weird Mysteries of the World*. Between the two, I became immediately insufferable, a constant fountain of summarized information, some of it funny, some of it downright grave, some of it approaching relevance, but most of it utterly trivial.

Trivia stuck to me. My head became a crowded and untamed jungle as the years passed, with facts seeping in to push aside more practical information. This book, the product of several months of trivial pursuit, so to speak, has been cathartic. If I could only write a trivia book on every place in the world (and a few places outside of it), I might be cured.

Overall, Ontario has more the feeling of a legal jurisdiction—slapped together for political or economic convenience—than a province. What do I mean? Culturally, Americans often note that Toronto more closely resembles the Great Lakes cities of Chicago, Detroit or Cleveland than it does Halifax or Edmonton.

It has been proposed that Toronto become a separate province. Indeed, Toronto often seems a different world, only faintly aware of the presence of Ontario. Urban-planning theorist Jane Jacobs seriously proposed that Toronto become semi-autonomous, and former mayor Mel Lastman once mused bombastically—a unique Lastman talent—about declaring a "Province of Toronto." (Not that the public has shown much interest in this. A man named Paul Lewin turned it into a platform in his candidacy for mayor in 2003. It won him only 271 votes.)

As well, the mid-sized industrial cities of Ontario, such as Windsor, Hamilton or Oshawa, seem not unlike U.S. places such as Flint, Bethlehem or Allentown. No surprise, considering that most of Ontario's first English-speaking citizens were Americans who arrived as Loyalists after the American Revolution. Although, Susannah Moodie's *Roughing It in the Bush* attests, most were not particularly loyal; they were generally poor and more motivated by offers of free land, farm equipment and cash bonuses.

Francophone areas of eastern Ontario feel closer to Québec. Ottawa seems half its own universe and half a quiet, suburban outgrowth of Montréal. The vast north of the province, with its logging and mining, feels closer to northern Québec or Manitoba. Although the Great Lakes make a convenient southern border, the shape of the province seems to almost deliberately disrespect cultures, languages, bio-regions, geographical features and economies.

As a result, the existence of a provincial identity is unheard of in Ontario.

And yet, here it is, the most populous province in the country, the centre of Canada's economy and cultural industry, and the number one destination in the country for immigrants.

So what's so trivial about all this? Only that out of this story, out of the absurdness and inherent contradictions, has come a tremendous supply of facts and history, eccentricities, funny anecdotes and oddities. Imagine the variety of tales that could come from a province drawn in all directions at once. Between all these, there are impressive achievements and famous names.

Here is a selection of facts that I flushed out or dug up. I hope you enjoy reading this collection as much as I enjoyed researching and writing it.

# JUST THE FACTS

*Give us a land of lakes*
*And a land of snow,*
*And we will build Ontario,*
*A place to stand,*
*A place to grow,*
*Ontar-i-ar-i-ar-i-o*

—Theme song to Ontario Pavilion, Expo '67, by Dolores Claman

**Across the Province**
At 1,076,395 km², Ontario is the second-largest province in Canada after Québec (Prince Edward Island could fit into it 190 times, with room to spare). That's a lot of space—much more than most Ontarians will come close to seeing in their lives, since much of the province is inaccessible by car.

More than 90 percent of the province's 12.5 million people live in the densely populated south. Nearly two-thirds of Ontario's population lives in the "Golden Horseshoe" area surrounding Toronto—and that amounts to one in every four Canadians!

DID YOU KNOW?

The name "Ontario" is believed to come from either of two Iroquois words, *kanadario*, meaning "sparkling water," or *onitariio*, meaning "beautiful lake." It originally referred to Lake Ontario and then gradually became applied to larger and larger areas of adjacent land. It did not become the province's formal name until Confederation in 1867.

## Loyal She Began, Loyal She Remains

That's Ontario's motto (*Ut Incepit Fidelis Sic Permanet*), a reference to the role played by United Empire Loyalists who settled in the province after the American Revolution (1775–83). It's been said that the policy of rewarding Americans with land if they moved to Canada was the only good thing King George III ever did. During George's bummer of a reign, the British government push the Americans into open rebellion, only to lose the Revolutionary War. The king spent his last 10 years locked in his palace grounds, out of his mind, talking to trees for hours on end and claiming to see angels.

### It's Legal

If you picked a bouquet of trilliums, Ontario's provincial flower, it's okay, you're not a criminal (unless you picked them from a protected park or someone else's lawn)! A popular myth says that it's illegal to pick trilliums in Ontario because of their official status. In reality, there is no such Ontario law—though picking them is illegal in British Columbia and a number of American states, because these flowers reproduce slowly.

O.Ont.! This guttural sounding group of letters refers to winners of the Order of Ontario, the province's most prestigious award. Since 1986, it has been given to Ontario's most notable citizens, including news anchor Knowlton Nash, author Jane Jacobs and golfer Mike Weir, entitling them to place "O.Ont." at the end of their names. The province gives out three other awards:

- ☞ The Ontario Medal for Good Citizenship
- ☞ The Ontario Medal for Police Bravery
- ☞ The Ontario Medal for Firefighters' Bravery.

# Official Bird

Thanks to the Avian Emblem Act of 1994, Ontario's official bird is the common loon. The loon—found across Canada, the northern United States and northern Europe—is popular. It's also the national bird of Canada (not the Canada goose) and the state bird of Minnesota.

### Thanks, Tree!

Since 1984, Ontario's official arboreal emblem has been the eastern white pine. Pines played a huge role in southern Ontario's logging industry in the late 19th century (when logging was the province's number one employer). However, the forests grew back mostly deciduous, and white pines are rarely seen in southern Ontario today.

# Official Tartan

Ontario has an official tartan (most Canadians would be surprised to learn that every province has one). It's blue and green to symbolize the forests and waters of the province.

# Franco-Flag

Since 2001, Franco-Ontarians have had their own official flag. It shows a fleur-de-lis (that's a lily, *en anglais)* and a trillium. The green and white background symbolizes the diversity of climate in Ontario.

# Coat of Arms

Ontario is the only province in Canada with a stylized coat of arms (its elements are shown in block shapes, instead of naturalistically). It features some of the better-known wildlife of northern Ontario: a moose, a deer and a black bear. It also displays the provincial crest, with three maple leaves under the English flag.

### Water, Water Everywhere

The human body is around 60 percent water. Ontario, on the other hand, is only 14.7 percent water (but that's still a lot—it takes up 158,654 km$^2$).

# LAY OF THE LAND

*"If some countries have too much history,
we have too much geography."*

—William Lyon Mackenzie King, Prime Minister. Born Kitchener, Ontario.

## Drowning in Lake Superior Not A Gas

Lake Superior—like all of the Great Lakes—is famous for its shipwrecks. The last major wreck in the Great Lakes, in 1975, was immortalized in Orillia, Ontario native Gordon Lightfoot's song, "The Wreck of the Edmund Fitzgerald." The line in that song, "They say that the lake never gives up her dead," refers to the unusual depth and low temperatures of Lake Superior. In other bodies of water, sunken corpses usually return to the surface because stomach contents ferment and produce gas that increases buoyancy. According to popular belief at least, the temperatures in Lake Superior remain too cold for fermentation to take place.

### DID YOU KNOW?

People often call Lake Superior the biggest lake in the world—but to be exact, it's the biggest freshwater lake by surface area in the world. So let's say it's superior with qualifications. Lake Baikal in Russia is bigger by volume, whereas the Caspian Sea, which geographers consider a lake, is bigger in both surface area and volume, although it is salt water.

Like many of Lightfoot's most popular songs, other bands frequently cover "The Wreck of the Edmund Fitzgerald." Toronto group the Sin-Tones even popularized a surf rock version!

## Niagara Falls—Spectacular, But Not the Biggest

Probably the most lucrative tourist destination in Ontario and the best-known waterfall in the world, Niagara Falls is the largest waterfall by volume in North America. It is often incorrectly billed as being the largest in the world.

☞ Victoria Falls, between Zambia and Zimbabwe, is the widest waterfall in the world.
☞ Boyoma Falls in the Democratic Republic of Congo (formerly Zaire) is the largest waterfall by volume.
☞ Angel Falls in Venezuela is the highest.
☞ Yosemite Falls in the United States is the highest waterfall in North America and Della Falls in British Columbia is the highest in Canada.

Niagara Falls is made up of three parts: American Falls and Bridal Veil Falls in New York State and the much larger Horseshoe Falls in Ontario. The *Maid of the Mist*—the ship that offers tourists a closer look of the falls—has been operating (as a series of different vessels) since 1846.

## DID YOU KNOW?

Pelee Island in Lake Erie is the southernmost inhabited place in Canada, located farther south than the northern border of California. Really! Check it out on a map. Pelee was originally several rocky islands connected by a marsh. Its name means "barren" in French. However, in the 19th century, the marsh was drained into a Dutch-style network of canals and dikes, creating a remote but excellent piece of farmland. The first vineyards and wine production in Canada happened on Pelee Island in the 1860s. It is known as having Ontario's mildest climate, though it is locked in by ice three months of the year.

The prize for the southernmost point in Canada goes to uninhabited Middle Island, just south of Pelee. Middle Island was once home to a lighthouse and its keeper, and during American Prohibition provided smugglers with a depot point for alcohol entering the United States. It has recently become part of Point Pelee National Park.

# Great Snakes!

In the 1830s, American military officer Robert E. Lee, who later became leader of the Confederate forces in the American Civil War, visited Pelee Island and killed its lighthouse keeper, apparently during a brawl. After returning to the U.S., he wrote a letter to the Canadian authorities, blaming the lighthouse keeper for starting the fight and describing him as "irascible and full of venom." He may have been referencing Pelee's earlier name, Isle aux Serpentes Sonnettes, or the Island of Poisonous Snakes.

### Guess They Didn't Have Time to Count Them

The picturesque Thousand Islands in the St. Lawrence River (actually, there are 1865 of them) have long been popular tourist destinations. Legend says mythical giant Paul Bunyan, who was contracted to dig the St. Lawrence River, built the islands. When his employer didn't pay him, he started to fill the river back in again. After a thousand (or maybe 1865) shovels of dirt, his employer relented and gave him the money.

Thousand Island salad dressing is actually a product of the American side, invented by the wife of a local tour guide around 1900.

The legend of Paul Bunyan may have developed from, and certainly incorporated elements of, the tall tales about Joseph Montferrand (called Big Joe Mufferaw in English), a francophone Ottawa Valley lumberjack. All kinds of feats were attributed to Montferrand, including building mountains and rivers and fighting dozens of men at once. He was particularly loved for standing up to the English logging company bosses. A statue is dedicated to Montferrand in his hometown of Mattawa, and Stompin' Tom Connors wrote a song about him. The name "Bunyan" may come from *bonyenne*, an expression of surprise or amazement.

## Sleeping In…Lake Superior, That Is

Sleeping Giant peninsula in Lake Superior, close to Thunder Bay, resembles a huge figure lying on its back. According to an Ojibwa legend, the giant is named Nanabijou, the Spirit of the Deep Sea Water. He turned to stone when Europeans discovered the location of nearby Silver Islet, which contained a rich silver mine that was a source of great wealth to the Ojibwa. The mine is said to be cursed and is now unusable, having been by the lake.

### It's Like the Thousand Islands—Times Thirty!

The St. Lawrence River's Thousand Islands have nothing numerically on the Thirty Thousand Islands of Georgian Bay. In this case, it's an overestimate—they actually number only around 17,500. Like the Thousand Islands, the Thirty Thousand Islands are now mostly protected as a national park.

### The Lost Villages

In 1959, the St. Lawrence Seaway opened. Flooding the St. Lawrence River allowed larger shipping to enter the Great Lakes. However, it also destroyed a number of towns in eastern Ontario. Mille Roches, Moulinette, Wales, Dickinson's

Landing, Farran's Point, Aultsville and the smaller hamlets of Maple Grove, Santa Cruz, Woodlands and Sheik's Island were all submerged. Residents were resettled into two new towns, Ingleside and Long Sault. Today, the old towns are memorialized in the Lost Villages Museum in Long Sault.

 Manitoulin Island in Lake Huron is the world's largest island in a freshwater lake. It contains 108 lakes in itself (some of which have their own islands)! The largest of the lakes, Lake Manitou, not surprisingly, lays claim to being the largest lake on a freshwater island in the world. *Manitoulin* means "spirit island" in the Ojibwa language.

**Famous for…Nothing**
Lake Doré, close to Pembroke, has an odd claim to fame. It is the largest lake in North America (or possibly the world) containing no islands.

# The Other Mississippi

The "Old Man River" has a cousin. The relatively large Mississippi River—totally unrelated to the more famous American river that shares its name—flows through eastern Ontario. Its name may be a corruption of the Algonquian word *mazinawzeebi*, meaning "painted image river" and referring to pictographs along its shores.

DID YOU KNOW?

Georgian Bay is home to the world's largest freshwater beach. Wasaga Beach is 14.5 kilometres long (and constantly crowded with Toronto tourists through most of the summer).

# Highs and Lows

Ontario's highest point is the rather ignominious Ishpatina Ridge, a remote line of hills north of Sudbury. It is the third lowest provincial high point in Canada (only Nova Scotia and Prince Edward Island's highest points are lower) and at 693 meters above sea level, it pales compared to the 5959-metre Mount Logan in the Yukon, Canada's highest point. For the record, Lake Ontario is the province's lowest point at sea level.

### Devilish Geography

The Devil's Punchbowl is a waterfall near Hamilton. Caledon also has a Devil's Pulpit Valley. Many of Ontario's hellish names were criticisms of their inhabitants. Brimstone, in the Devil's Pulpit, started off as a rough mining town. It got its name from the pious citizens of nearby Belfountain, who thought it might be a warning to the drinking and swearing miners. It's not known what the miners thought about the villagers—but you can guess some names that they might have given to Belfountain.

# Switching Teams

In three billion years of geological history, Ontario has been part of five different continents: Arctica, Nena, Rodinia, Pangaea and, of course, North America.

### Grenville Mountains

You may have never heard of the Grenville Mountains (even if you live on them!), but that's okay—they were a bit before your time. They formed in southern Ontario 1.3 billion years ago and were as high as the Himalayas. Over time, they wore down to almost nothing and today form the Canadian Shield.

# Rock of Ages

The oldest rock found in Ontario is located near Kenora and dates back 3.18 billion years.

DID YOU  KNOW?

Geologists consider Toronto's Scarborough the best record of the last ice age in North America. Layers of sediment exposed on the cliffs provide an almost complete record of each stage of glaciation.

### The Mysterious Lake On the Mountain

Imagine taking a dip in a lake while looking down over another lake below! Prince Edward County's Lake on the Mountain is a deep lake on top of a hill, with a water level 62 metres higher than Lake Ontario, which is at the bottom of the hill. The lake has a constant flow of fresh water from a source yet to be determined.

Mohawks called it the Lake of the Gods. Some early settlers cut a stream from the lake down into Lake Ontario, using the energy to power a mill—one of the earliest industrial developments in Ontario.

### Are We in Ontario or Not?

Ontario's northwestern boundary was not established until 1899. Previously it fluctuated between Thunder Bay and Winnipeg, and at one point ran through Kenora (known at the time as Rat Portage). Both Manitoba and Ontario claimed the town, and residents were allowed to vote in both provinces' elections. The conflict caused confusion and disputes about liquor laws—for a time, liquor was legal on the Ontario side but banned on the Manitoba side. Want to come over to this side of town for a drink?

# WEATHER OR NOT

## The Shocking Truth About Willie(s)

Ontario's meteorologically gifted albino groundhog, Wiarton Willie, has been predicting when winter will end since 1956. Mac McKenzie, an assistant to the provincial health minister at the time, brought the custom to the small Georgian Bay town of Wiarton. The concept of Groundhog Day seems to have developed in Pennsylvania, where Punxsutawney Phil began his tenure as resident rodent sage in 1887. It was originally derived from Hedgehog Day, an ancient festival celebrated on February 2 in several European countries. Today, Wiarton Willie attracts 20,000 tourists and generates $750,000 in income for the town annually. He is the subject of a solemn stone statue overlooking Wiarton's beach, among other tributes. More recently, other towns have tried to capitalize on the craze, including Gary the Groundhog in Kleinburg, Ontario, Shubenacadie Sam in Nova Scotia and Balzac Billy in Alberta.

In 1999, it was discovered, just days before he was to make his famous appearance, that Wiarton Willie was dead. The town quickly arranged an elaborate open casket funeral to be held in place of Groundhog Day. Scandal ensued when it was revealed that the groundhog in the casket was not the dearly beloved Willie, but another long-dead stuffed groundhog. Willie himself, who had passed away in early hibernation, was too badly decomposed to be publicly displayed. Of course, a number of rodents have played the role of official groundhog since the festival began. Today Wiarton publicly reveals that there are two in active service—appropriately named Willie I and Willie II.

Punxsutawney Phil, on the other hand—at least according to his handlers—is immortal, and was born at some point before 1887.

LATE BREAKING NEWS!
In July 2006, another "Willie" departed for the great burrow in the sky. His handlers again held a funeral, but this Willie was cremated.

**Lightning Never Strikes Twice—It Strikes 72 Times**
The CN Tower in Toronto is struck by lightning on average 72 times per year. In high winds, the tower tip can sway up to 1.07 metres. The tower is built to withstand an earthquake up to 8.5 on the Richter scale. A fault line extends through the St. Lawrence River and Lake Ontario, and sometimes produces small earthquakes in Québec.

**DID YOU  KNOW?**

In 1954, Hurricane Hazel, t]  rst storm of the season,
and one of the few hurricanes to make it so far inland, devastated southern Ontario. Starting in the Caribbean, it struck
the North Carolina coast, crossed the continent and passed
directly through Toronto, causing the Don and Humber
Rivers to flood. A number of bridges were washed out, low-
lying neighbourhoods destroyed and 83 people killed, making
it the deadliest-known hurricane in Canadian history. Bodies
continued to wash up on the New York side of Lake Ontario
days later. At the time, it was reported to have caused $25
million in damages. North of Toronto, it overwhelmed the
dike and canal system of Holland Marsh, located below sea
level, and left the farming area submerged. After Hazel, parts
of Toronto had to be completely rebuilt. Dramatic changes
were made in drainage systems for Ontario rivers.

The flat and dry plains of southwestern Ontario are known for tornadoes, and five of the 10 most deadly hurricanes in Canada have occurred in Ontario. The worst in the province was the June 17, 1946, tornado that struck Windsor, killing 17 people and wounding hundreds.

## Thanks, Hurricane

Ontario's first recorded hurricane occurred on June 30, 1792, in Niagara County, between Port Robertson and Fontill. Conveniently, it cleared a path through the forest connecting the two villages. A street later built there was named Hurricane Road.

## The Storm of Storms

Lake Huron was hit with the "Storm of Storms" in 1913. Also known as the "Black Sunday Storm," the six-day-long squall sunk 34 ships and killed 270 sailors.

### Toronto's Worst Snowfall

Toronto had its worst single-day snowfall in 1944, when 48 centimetres came down. Twenty-one people died. The army, busy in Europe, was not called in.

### Extremes

The coldest ever recorded temperature in Ontario is –58.3°C in Iroquois Falls, near Timmins in 1935. The warmest is 42.2°C in Biscotasing, near Sault Ste. Marie in 1919. On average, Windsor has the warmest temperature, in Ontario and Winisk, on Hudson Bay, has the coldest.

# GHOST STORIES

Ontario may be Canada's most haunted province. It certainly has a lot of history, including a lot of bad memories. Nearly every building over a century in age, and even some newer ones, seem to have ghost stories associated with them.

### Niagara-on-the-Lake
It's fitting that Ontario's first capital and one of its oldest towns should be the province's per capita ghost leader. The town has dozens of stories of hauntings.

### Olde Angel Inn
The Inn—one of the oldest in Ontario—is supposed to be haunted by the ghost of Captain Colin Swayze, a British soldier who served during the War of 1812. Swayze slipped away from the retreating army to visit his girlfriend and was beaten to death by American soldiers in the basement of the Inn. Swayze is often heard walking around late at night, but legend says that as long as the British flag flies over the Inn (as it still does), the ghost will be harmless.

### Shaw House
This house was destroyed in the War of 1812, but the sound of crying sometimes can be heard on the site where it stood. Supposedly this is Sophia Shaw, fiancée of Isaac Brock, commander of the British forces in Ontario, crying after his death.

### Fort George
Many people claim to have seen ghosts at Niagara-on-the-Lake's historic Fort George, including apparitions of a girl, a soldier, an old woman, an old man and furniture moving. Strange noises have also been heard. At least one person claims to have been chased by a gang of ghosts.

# The Ghost of Red Emma?

Some believe that the ghost of early 20th-century anarchist labour organizer Emma Goldman haunts the former Labour Lyceum in Toronto, where she often gave speeches. When she died in 1940, her body was put on display there for nearly a week and was visited by thousands of people wanting to see and touch her before she was buried. Goldman was Jewish—albeit far from religious—and Jewish custom normally requires that people be buried within a day of death and not be touched by anyone other than a rabbi. The Labour Lyceum later moved and the old building became a Chinese restaurant. Patrons often reported seeing the ghostly figure of a woman, hovering in a reclined position, in what is now the women's washroom. The Chinese owners of the building—mindful of the bad effects a ghost might have on their business—hired a feng shui expert, who advised them to move the front entrance and erect lions around the doorways to improve the building's energy. Sightings of the ghost stopped.

An alternative story about the building is that it was briefly a Chinese funeral home before becoming a restaurant, and some say that the ghost appeared to be a Chinese woman.

### Gibraltar Point Lighthouse

The ghost of its first keeper—a former German teacher named John Paul Rademüller—supposedly haunts Toronto Island's lighthouse. He was a moonshiner, and in 1815, when he refused to sell liquor to two already drunk soldiers from the garrison, they beat him to death. The soldiers cut up the keeper's body and buried him near the lighthouse. Rademüller's ghost has been seen walking up the steps of the lighthouse and stumbling around, apparently searching for his missing limbs. Human bones were dug up near the lighthouse in 1893.

## Fort York

Ghosts of a soldier, a distraught woman and a mysterious man dressed in green haunt Fort York, the site of three bloody battles during the War of 1812.

## Soldier's Tower

The ghost of Ivan Reznikoff, a Russian stone mason, haunts the tower at the University of Toronto. Reznikoff died in a fight with a co-worker during construction of the tower. He apparently fell from the tower to his death and was buried on the spot by his rival, who then disappeared.

## Royal Ontario Museum (ROM)

Several ghost stories come from the ROM. Some people have sighted the museum's first director wandering in a nightshirt in the Chinese galleries, whereas others claim to have seen the ghost of a little girl, nicknamed Celeste, in the (no longer existing) Planetarium wing. A child's stone sarcophagus in the Roman gallery is supposed to sometimes produce a strange, cold wind.

### Colborne Lodge

The ghost of Jemima, wife of architect John Howard, haunts their home, Colborne Lodge (now part of High Park in Toronto). She is seen peering out the second-floor window, where she apparently stood during the last days of her life. Jemima died after a long period of illness, sedated on opium, looking out at her already-constructed grave next to the house.

### Mackenzie House

Many people have reported seeing the ghost of rebellious newspaper editor William Lyon Mackenzie (grandfather of Prime Minister Mackenzie King) in his Toronto townhouse, which is now a museum dedicated to him. Taps have been said to go off and on by themselves, while toilets have engaged in unassisted flushing—both odd, considering that the house had no indoor plumbing in Mackenzie's time.

## Château Laurier

Ottawa's famous hotel, the Château Laurier, may be haunted. The spirit is believed to be Charles Melville Hays, the head of the Grand Trunk Railway, which built the hotel. Hays drowned on the *Titanic*, just before the hotel was to open. He is seen in a dark coat on the hotel's fifth floor and is sometimes heard whistling.

## Fulford Mansion

Senator George Taylor Fulford—who had made his fortune peddling "Dr. William's Pink Pills for Pale People"—built Fulford House in Brockville. His wife, who in life was fanatically afraid of storms, apparently haunts the house. She is heard screaming and pounding on the outside of the door, demanding to be let in out of the rain.

**Brampton Jail**

The ghostly figure of a woman holding a child appears once a year, standing outside the old Brampton Jail, looking up to a window—possibly to her husband. Remains of executed prisoners have been found buried in the jail's former exercise yard. In fact, at one point, Ontario's laws said that all executed prisoners had to be buried on prison grounds.

## And For My Next Trick...

Every Halloween, until 1995, fans of escape artist Harry Houdini gathered at the Harry Houdini Magical Hall of Fame in Niagara Falls to seek his reincarnation. In 1995, the museum burned down, destroying many of the props and escape-trick materials kept there. Some people believed it was the doing of Houdini's ghost—he had demanded that all of his tricks be burned after his death to conceal his secrets, but his brother, who inherited them, sold them to be publicly displayed.

# OTHER STRANGE PHENOMENA

## The Baldoon Mystery

Deeply wrapped in old Ontario folklore is the frightening "Baldoon Mystery." The incident took place in a small, now non-existent, Scottish settlement near Wallaceburg called Baldoon. In 1829, a settler named John Macdonald and his family built a house there, but strange forces immediately assaulted it. Beams from the barn roof fell onto farm workers below. Stones and musket balls appeared from nowhere, flying at the house and smashing its windows. The Macdonalds and their friends would collect the balls, only to have them disappear. Water mysteriously poured out of the ceiling of the house, and fires would break out for no reason. The family's barn mysteriously burned down. Pots and knives flew through the air.

Re Nah Sawa, an aboriginal man who visited the farm at the time, is recorded in local papers saying: "J.T. McDonald purchased a piece of land which the disturbers wanted to purchase and these are the steps they took to have revenge on him. I saw his corn and it did not grow more than a foot high that year, and his crops were all destroyed. We called them 'wild Indians' in our language and we believe they made their abode in the prairie southeast of the house on the farm. We were aware of their doings and tried to tell him what we knew about them, but could not understand each other's language."

In the end—after an unsuccessful exorcism and other attempts at removing the ghost—Macdonald went to a friend of the family, who had experience with the supernatural. She told him that it was the doing of an old woman who lived in a nearby log house. The old woman could transform herself into a goose with a black head, and she could only be stopped with a silver bullet. Macdonald recognized the description of the woman and recalled seeing a goose wandering around. He found the goose on his farm and shot it in the wing with a silver bullet. After that, we went to the old woman's house and found that she had a wound on her arm.

At that point, the incidents stopped, or at least the story stops. Unfortunately for fans of the paranormal, there seems to be no information on what became of the old woman.

## Our Lady of Marmora
Although deliberately not publicized, numerous people claim to have seen an apparition of the Virgin Mary in a field near Marmora. Among them is the American actor Yaphet Kotto (star of the *Homicide Life on the Street* series) who recently moved to Marmora as a landed immigrant.

# The Scottish Play

The Grand Opera House, once Toronto's main theatre, was
built in 1875. It burned down in 1879 during the performance
of a certain Shakespearean play. (Actors consider speaking the
name of the play to be bad luck.) The theatre was rebuilt
shortly afterwards, and later was the site of one of Canada's
most famous mysteries, the disappearance of Ambrose Small.

# Ambrose Small

On December 2, 1919, Canada's leading theatre magnate,
Ambrose Small, disappeared after suddenly selling his theatres and depositing the cash—$1.5 million dollars—into
the bank. He was last seen leaving the Grand Opera House,
after meeting there with his lawyer. A police investigation
and media storm ensued, but Small was never found. In
1960, the case was formally closed. The Grand Opera House
is now gone—only remembered in the name Grand Opera
Lane, an alley in Toronto's Financial District. Small's ghost
is said to haunt two of his theatres: the Grand Theatre in
London and the Tivoli Theatre in Hamilton.

# MY WAY OR THE HIGHWAY

## Why It Takes So Long to Get to Work

The 401 Highway (officially named the Macdonald-Cartier Freeway), stretching from Windsor to the Québec border, is the busiest highway in North America, by daily numbers of cars. Its traffic count recently surpassed the Santa Monica Freeway in California. Where it passes through Toronto, the 401 averages more than 425,000 vehicles per day! That's a lot of time stuck in traffic. The 401 is also the busiest truck route in North America. That's no surprise, considering that Windsor is the world's busiest commercial border crossing.

# It's a Long Story at Least

Yonge Street is widely described as the longest street in the world, but is it really? Or is this just something the Toronto tourism department made up? It all depends on your definition of just what Yonge Street is.

The street begins at Lake Ontario and forms one of the main arterials in Toronto. North of Toronto, it used to become Highway 11, stretching all the way north to Kapuskasing and west to the Minnesota border at Rainy River. (At that point, it connected with the unrelated Minnesota State Highway 11.) But was northern Ontario's Highway 11 actually part of Yonge Street? That all depended on who you asked. A monument at Dundas Square in Toronto labelling Younge as the world's longest street leaves little room for doubt. But residents of Highway 11 through northern Ontario, however, were less keen to be associated with Toronto's main street. Between North Bay and Cochrane, it was originally known as the Ferguson Highway (after Premier George Howard Ferguson) and is now part of the Trans-Canada Highway.

In the 1990s, the waters were muddied further when the Conservative government offloaded responsibility for a number of provincial roads onto regions and municipalities. The stretch of Highway 11 between Toronto and Barrie became a local road. It is now Highway 1 where it passes through York Region and Highway 4 in Simcoe County. For most of that way, road signs also label it as Yonge Street, although it is briefly known as Bridge Street and Barrie Street near the town of Bradford. In Barrie, it disappears altogether for some way before restarting north of the city as the old Highway 11.

No records nor lists seem to have been made on the subject (despite what people say, the *Guinness Book of World Records* does not include it).

## DID YOU KNOW?

It is ironic that Toronto's most famous street is named after a man who never set foot in the city and had virtually no connection to it. Understandably, few Torontonians have ever heard of him. Sir George Yonge, Fifth Baronet of Culliton (1731–1812), was the British Secretary of War when the surveying of Yonge Street started in 1794. He later became Master of the Mint and Governor of the Cape of Good Hope (at the southern tip of Africa). John Graves Simcoe, the rather autocratic and eccentric first lieutenant-governor of Ontario, who was a personal friend of Sir George, chose the name.

**Simcoe Day? No, Really!**
Few Ontario residents know the official name given in the province to the August civic holiday. Do you need an excuse for a day off? In Toronto, the Saturday of the long weekend is Caribana, a massive Caribbean carnival that is the biggest street party in North America. The day of parades and partying has been around since 1967, but still finds difficulty gaining acceptance with certain stodgy Torontonians. It was once held on Yonge Street, but complaints pushed it away from populated areas to Lakeshore Boulevard.

# There Once Was a Highway Sign in Toronto...

Lighted signs overhang the highways in Toronto, notifying drivers if the road ahead is busy, if lanes are closed or if storms are predicted. Sometimes, when there's less to say, they are forums for poetry. "Check your gauges, control your rages" and "Why fool with fate? Don't tailgate!" are some of the zingers penned by budding poets in the city's Traffic Management Department.

More inspirational messages come from the flashing Inglis Appliance sign, near the Gardiner Expressway in Toronto. Drivers are treated to phrases such as: "The greatest remedy for anger is delay." Inglis—a long-time industrial fixture in Toronto that once employed 17,000 people—moved to Mississauga in 1981. In 1987, American company Whirlpool acquired majority ownership. The sign sits on top of the abandoned Inglis factory and the messages are electronically transmitted from the company's offices.

**DID YOU**  **KNOW?**

The eternal question in the minds of pedestrians does: pushing the button actually a make a difference in bringing on the walk signal? Every city has its own system. In Toronto, pressing the button is necessary to change a signal where a busy street meets a minor one. (Drivers unknowingly do the same thing—the signals change when their car passes over a sensor.) In places where two busy streets meet, however, the traffic light patterns are controlled by a computerized system and pressing a button has no effect.

Ontario's first 178 license plates were issued in 1903. They were made out of leather, and had aluminum lettering.

## A Smooth Ride

Ontario's first concrete highway, between Toronto and Hamilton, was built between 1911 and 1915. It was a mere 5.5 metres wide—two lanes. Today the 401 has 16 lanes at its widest point.

## Hitchhikers' Hell

Just about anyone who has ever hitchhiked between Ontario and western Canada will recoil in horror at the name of Wawa, the principal town between Sault Ste. Marie and Thunder Bay. Known otherwise for its giant metal goose, Wawa has a reputation as a place where it's easy to hitchhike in but hard to thumb a ride out. Although no statistics are kept on this, numerous anecdotes report people waiting help-lessly for days by the side of the road and even waving money in the air in the desperate hope of getting a lift out of the town. Is it the goose that spooks drivers? Or the mosquitoes?

## Not Much Cover

Ontario has only one remaining covered bridge. Built in 1881, it crosses the Grand River at West Montrose, near Elmira, and is locally nicknamed the "Kissing Bridge"—not a bad thing to do while you're waiting for the rain to stop.

 Nearly all major roads in southern Ontario are part of the concession system, an elaborate and unusual grid drawn up in surveys during the late 18th and early 19th centuries. Based on the shoreline of the nearest lake or river, a number of different grids stretch inland, sometimes meshing awkwardly with each other at different angles. The first road parallel to the lake is often called the baseline or the first concession. Roads perpendicular from the lake are called lines or side roads. Every road is 2 kilometres apart. In Toronto, where Queen Street is the old first concession (and originally the northern boundary of the city), Bloor Street is 2 kilometres north, followed by St. Clair Avenue and then Eglinton Avenue.

DID YOU KNOW?

The farthest place north you can drive to year-round in Ontario is Central Patricia, at the end of Highway 599, some 528 kilometres north of Thunder Bay.

# RIDING OUT OF TOWN ON A RAIL

## An Elephant Is Never Forgotten

On September 15, 1885, Jumbo, Barnum & Bailey Circus' giant African elephant, was killed instantly as he was led across train tracks while the show was camped in St. Thomas. An unscheduled express train hit the elephant from behind, overturning the engine and two cars. In 1985, St. Thomas unveiled a full-sized statue of the elephant to honour the 100th anniversary of this tragic death.

Jumbo was billed as the world's biggest elephant. Comparisons of Jumbo to other big things led to a well-worn adjective, as in "jumbo jet," "jumbo popcorn" or that famous oxymoron, "jumbo shrimp." Jumbo got his name from people mispronouncing *jambo*, the Swahili word for "hello."

**DID YOU KNOW?**

The fastest train in Canada is VIA Rail's Train 66 between Toronto and Montréal. It runs the 520-kilometre route in three hours and 44 minutes. European and Japanese express trains run faster.

## It Didn't Get Off the Ground

Although airplanes weren't invented until 1903, Ontario had an "air line" in 1871! That's according to the railway definition of the term, at least. An "air line" is a long, completely straight stretch of track that gives an exceptionally fast ride. From Glencoe to Fort Erie, the Canada Air Line, run by the Great Western Railway, measured over 230 kilometres.

The only monorail system in the province, at the Toronto Zoo, was abruptly shut down and dismantled after an accident in 1994. One train lost power and rolled backwards into another train while passing through the "Canadian Domain" section of the zoo. Luckily no passengers fell into the wolf or grizzly enclosures nearby, though quite a few people were badly hurt in the accident. The monorail was replaced with the "Zoomobile," a tractor-pulled bus.

**DID YOU KNOW?**

In 1916, railway workers burning brush near Matheson in northern Ontario sparked what became known as the Great Fire. It destroyed 1300 km² of land, including six villages. Two other villages were also damaged and 223 people were killed in the blaze.

ONLY IN
ONTARIO

Feel like taking a canoe trip? Can't get there by car? One the features of Ontario Northland, the provincially owned railway company, is a canoe carriage. It is said to be the only one in the world—holding up to 18 canoes or kayaks for tourists heading north. Ontario Northland is best known for the Polar Bear Express train, running from Cochrane to Moosonee near the shores of James Bay.

# ROW, ROW, ROW YOUR BOAT

The Trent-Severn Waterway is Ontario's longest canal, connecting a number of lakes and rivers and stretching 386 kilometres from Trenton to Georgian Bay. It has 45 locks and took 87 years to complete. In fact, when it was finished in 1920, it was almost useless to industry, because it was narrow and trains had become the preferred mode of transportation. Pleasure boating into cottage country has been its main use. The waterway passes through Balsam Lake, 256.3 metres above sea level, which is the highest place in the world that a boat can be navigated into from sea level.

The Welland Canal, connecting Lake Ontario with Lake Erie, is the only Ontario canal still used for industrial shipping. It allows tankers to bypass Niagara Falls to reach Detroit or Cleveland. Some 3000 ships bring 40 million tonnes of cargo through the canal annually. There are eight locks along the canal, each requiring about 91 million litres of water to lift ships to the next level.

**DID YOU KNOW?**

Every winter in Ottawa, the Rideau Canal becomes the world's longest ice rink, called the Skateway, with 7.8 kilometres cleared for skating (that's as big as 90 hockey rinks). It's not unheard of for students and downtown workers to commute to school or work by skate! However, because of global warming, the period of time the canal can be safely used for skating is constantly decreasing.

During the summer, the 202-kilometre long Rideau Canal, stretching from Kingston to Ottawa, is used for boating. It is the oldest continually used canal in North America and has 47 locks, more than any other canal in Ontario.

Construction of the canal started during the War of 1812 and it was designed as a military supply route, intended to get provisions from Montreal to Kingston. A war with the Americans would render the St. Lawrence River too dangerous for shipping.

## Jacques Cousteau's Underwater Adventures

Famous French underwater explorer Jacques Cousteau came to Lake Ontario in 1980 to explore the wrecks of the *Hamilton* and the *Scourge*, two sunken American ships near St. Catharines. The ships went down in a storm in 1813, and their wrecks were not discovered until 1975.

After their sinking, the *Hamilton* and the *Scourge* were far from forgotten. In fact, a popular legend says that on stormy nights, ghostly images of the ships would again appear on the surface of the water. Seeing the ships was said to have been a bad omen, possibly foreshadowing the death of one of your crew.

## Ferry Tales

Ferries were once a major feature of the Great Lakes, connecting towns and cities before roads or railways, or when the other options seemed impractical. Since the 19th century, Toronto has run ferries between the mainland and Toronto Islands. The ferries run year-round, bringing tourists to the island and carrying commuters to the mainland.

Other ferries have been less popular—and some of them have been downright ridiculous. One of the strangest ferries to cross Toronto Habour was the privately owned Tinning's Cigar Boat, a sort of paddlewheel that had the entire boat contained within the wheel. The inside of the boat, where the passengers sat, stayed steady, while the outside spun. As this description would suggest, the boat was a huge failure, especially when any type of waves came into the harbour.

## Call Me Ishmael

There are no white whales (or whales of any type) in Lake Ontario. Captain Ihab (Ihab Shaker, that is—an unfortunately named Egyptian immigrant who had earlier run a ferry across the Red Sea) attempted unsuccessfully to start a commercial communter ferry service in 1998. The ferry would have linked Toronto and its suburbs along the lakeshore.

# Bad Planning Killed the Cat

Attempts by the city of Rochester, New York, to restart an old ferry route between Toronto and Rochester—famously taken by Ernest Hemingway—have so far been a failure. Toronto was a reluctant partner in the deal. When the route began in 2004, passengers departed from a brand-new terminal in Rochester, but arrived at a tent in Toronto. Media pressure prompted the city to build a terminal of its own, only to have the service fail soon afterwards. The company originally contracted to run the ferry went bankrupt, but the ship—built in Australia and registered in the Bahamas—was bought by the city of Rochester itself. Rochester nicknamed the ferry "the Cat," unintentionally referencing the disastrous Vancouver Island "Sea Cat" ferries. It's unclear if the Rochester ferry will run again.

# PUTTING ON AIRS

## Wright On! The Island, That Is

Orville Wright, the American co-inventor of the airplane, bought Lambert Island in Georgian Bay and renamed it Wright Island. He spent most of his summers there.

 The first plane ever built in Ontario was nick-named "Jenny Canuck." She was manufactured at the Curtiss factory in Toronto in 1915.

 A.V. Roe Canada Ltd. built the famous Canadian Avro Arrow fighter aircraft in Malton, Ontario, in 1958. Prime Minister John Diefenbaker cancelled the Avro Arrow in 1959, under pressure from the United States.

## Toronto Pearson International Airport

Whatever you call it—it was previously known as "Lester B. Pearson International Airport" and before that "Toronto International Airport" and before that "Malton Airport"—Toronto's airport is busy. It is Canada's biggest airport, and the 29th biggest in the world, handling about 26 million passengers a year (that's about twice the population of Ontario). Pearson's parking lot holds 12,600 cars at once. It was first established as a small, local airport in 1939, and is actually mostly located in Mississauga, not Toronto. The much smaller Toronto City Centre Airport on Toronto Islands is the only airport completely within the city.

Pearson is also probably one of the world's only airports known for its wildlife. Deer, coyotes, foxes and rabbits have been spotted in its outer reaches, which include forested areas. The airport has a policy of not killing animals, so animal control officers try to scare the wildlife away from the runways with tactics such as pyrotechnics and loud, recorded noises. They've also tried giving interfering birds a taste of their own avian medicine. In 2000, the airport actually bought three peregrine falcons, which live on the roof of one of the buildings and prey on smaller birds.

## The Toronto Blessing

One of the stranger things to emerge from the mass of spaghetti junction highways, motels and warehouses around Pearson is the Toronto Airport Christian Fellowship. The plain-looking church now draws visitors from around the world, who spontaneously laugh, cry, writhe on the ground, swing imaginary swords—and claim to be healed of illnesses. Some have even sworn that their tooth cavities were instantly filled! The terms "Toronto Blessing" and the "Toronto Blessing Movement" have been coined to describe the phenomenon, which has spawned similar churches in other cities. Some rival (and probably less popular) churches have called the Toronto Blessing satanic.

# SETTLING DOWN

*Is it surprising that the French and British, eternally enemies, ruined each other's first settlements in Ontario? Some people just don't know how to get along.*

## Ste. Marie

The first European settlement in Ontario was Ste. Marie, started as a French Jesuit mission near modern-day Midland in 1639. It was abandoned in 1649 because it could not be defended against the Iroquois, who were allies of the British and enemies of the French.

## The Portable Capital

Ontario's capital wasn't always Toronto. It was originally Niagara-on-the-Lake, where the first session of Parliament was held outdoors in 1792. In 1796, Toronto, became the capital because Niagara-on-the-Lake was too close to the border and was thought to be vulnerable to an American attack. Between 1840 and 1867, Upper and Lower Canada (Ontario and Québec) were united into one province. The first capital was Kingston, but it later was moved to Montréal. After that, it alternated between Toronto and Québec City.

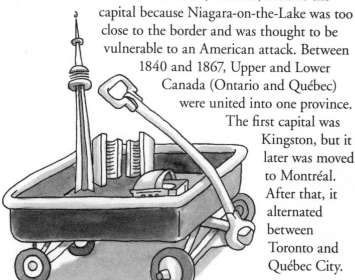

Finally, on advice from Queen Victoria, Ottawa was named the capital. After Confederation, when the provinces were divided again, Ottawa became the national capital and Toronto and Québec City regained their status as provincial capitals. No work shortages, it seems, for people who draw stars on maps.

**Moose Factory**
You might be surprised to learn that the oldest English-speaking settlement in Ontario is Moose Factory—built on an island in the Moose River, where it meets James Bay. The Hudson's Bay Company originally set up the town as a trading post in the 1670s. It was destroyed by the French in 1696, but reestablished several decades later.

DID YOU KNOW?

The towns of Spanish and Espanola, as well as the Spanish River, were named for a Spanish woman apparently captured by an Ojibwa expedition far into the south before Europeans moved into northern Ontario. The woman married an Ojibwa man and taught their children to speak Spanish. When French traders arrived in the area, they were amazed to find Spanish speakers living there. Espanola comes from the French word for "Spanish."

# The Name Game

Ever felt the need for a change? A chance to reinvent yourself? A number of Ontario cities have undergone name changes. Some have been the result of mergers and amalgamations, others because of popular trends or political pressure. See for yourself how the new names have changed their images.

| Current Name | Previous Name(s) |
| --- | --- |
| Toronto | York |
| Ottawa | Bytown |
| Windsor | Sandwich |
| Kitchener | Berlin |
| Brampton | Buffy's Corners |
| Belleville | Meyer's Creek |
| Brockville Buell's | Bay |
| Niagara-on-the-Lake | Newark |
| Thunder Bay | Merger of Port Arthur and Fort William |
| Peterborough | Scott's Plains |
| Cornwall | New Johnstown |
| Cambridge | Merger of Galt, Preston and Hespeler |
| Owen Sound | Sydenham |
| Sudbury | Sainte-Anne-des-Pins |
| Port Hope | Smith's Creek |
| St. Catharines | Shipman's Corners |

### Ich Bin Kein Berliner

Berlin, Ontario, was a mostly German settlement that once featured a statue of Kaiser Wilhelm I. But neither the name nor the statue survived the First World War. When British Field Marshall Horatio Kitchener drowned after his ship hit a German mine, people took revenge by tearing down the Kaiser's likeness and throwing it into the river. The city was renamed Kitchener (by a controversial referendum boycotted by most residents) and the statue was lost, possibly melted down to make armaments. In 1996, the German-Canadian Professional Business Association—who had paid for the statue to be put up in the first place—restored its pedestal, with a plaque telling the story of the missing Kaiser.

## Buffy the Sobriety Slayer

The first public building in modern-day Brampton was a pub called Buffy's Tavern. As the town grew, the settlement became known as Buffy's Corners. When the first church was built, its minister disagreed with the town being named after a pub and proposed the name of his hometown in northern England as a substitute.

# WEIRD PLACE NAMES

As the most populous province in Canada, it makes sense that Ontario has more settlements than any other part of the country. Ontario is also known for its proliferation of odd and unusual place names.

Some towns have welcoming names such as Friendly Corners, Sweets Corners, Sunshine, Hope, Utopia, Sunny Slope, Lively, Forward, Advance, Prospect, Harmony, Sparkle City, Honey Harbour, Eldorado, Eden, Garden of Eden, Hearts Desire, Happy Hollow, Happy Landing, Happy Valley and Happyland, not to mention the village of Welcome itself.

Others such as Crampton, Strange, Cultus, Teeterville, Feversham, Mono Mills, Wolverine Beach, Paincourt, Swastika, Lunge Lodge, Siberia, Slabtown, Brimstone, Wartburg, Hungerford, Hungry Hollow, Bummer's Roost, The Slash, Orwell and Go Home are less appealing.

Some recall much bigger and more famous cities such as London, Paris, Cairo, Athens, Moscow, Odessa, Warsaw, Boston, Washington, Damascus, Brussels, Zurich, Vienna, Orléans, Lyons, Manchester, Baltimore, Belfast, Dublin, Khartum, Delhi, Geneva, Lisbon, Melbourne, Brisbane, Perth and Cambridge.

Some are just plain bizarre, such as Electric, Emo, Oungah, Frogmore, Dogs Nest, Science Hill, Punkydoodle's Corners, Wanup, South Porcupine, Squirrel Town, Two O'Clock, Union Hall, Burpee, Propensity, Dinner Point Depot, Huckabones Corners, Buttermilk Falls, Cheeseborough, Jellyby, Whitebread, Tempo, Forget, Lo-Ellen, Biggles, Marsville, Peepabun, Kilbride, The Bush, Gasline, Turbine, Zenda, Dorking, Shakespeare and Merlin.

# CONFUSING PLACE NAMES

## The Other Paris: Two Degrees of Separation

Paris, a pretty town of 10,000 people on the Grand River, in southwestern Ontario, has little connection with the French capital. It is named after plaster of Paris, which the town is famous for producing. Plaster of Paris itself is named after the gypsum deposits originally mined to make it, first found near Paris, France.

### London, Ontario, or London, U.K.?

That's the question Ontario residents tend to ask if you say you're going to London. John Graves Simcoe, the first lieutenant-governor, promoted London, Ontario, as the provincial capital. He envisioned it as a duplicate of London, U.K., complete with the Thames River (which the Askunessippi River was renamed) and streets and neighbourhoods named after the original city. The vision—as you can guess—didn't exactly come to pass. Although London, Ontario, later became a city of nearly 500,000 people, its original remoteness prevented it from ever becoming the capital. Hockey player Eric Lindros and singer Guy Lombardo are natives of London—London, Ontario, that is.

## Two Heads are Better Than One

There is not one, but two villages in Ontario named Bond Head. Both are in honour of the notoriously authoritarian and unpopular (not to mention weirdly named) 19th-century lieutenant-general Sir Francis Bond Head. After making a number of enemies in the province (historians widely blame him for causing the 1837 Rebellion), he was fired and sent back to Britain. Bond Street in Toronto was likely named after him—ironic, considering that William Lyon Mackenzie, one of Bond's greatest opponents, lived on it.

DID YOU  KNOW?

Ontario's most popular place names? Eight villages are named Mount Pleasant, six named Salem, six Zion, six Maple Grove, five Pine Grove. You can't always be original.

### Imitated, but Never Duplicated

Ontario shares its name with a few other places. The best known is probably Ontario, California, a large suburb of Los Angles founded in 1882 by Brockville native George Chaffey and named after his home province. "Ontario, CA" is now home to over 100,000 people and an international airport—but is notorious for causing confusion with "Ontario, Canada." Chaffey was an engineer and a professional founder of planned cities. A number of successful communities in the United States and Australia owe their existence to him. The U.S. navy ship, the USS *George Chaffey*, is named in his honour.

A similar story explains the existence of Ontario, Oregon. Irishman James Virtue, who had previously lived near Enniskillen, Ontario, founded the Oregon town in 1883.

# Other Torontos

Toronto, too, has spawned a number of imitators. Toronto, Ohio, was named after the capital of Ontario. Today there are more than 5000 Torontoans (as opposed to Torontonians). Toronto, New South Wales, Australia, was named in honour of Toronto, Ontario), rowing champion Ned Hanlan who was touring Australia in 1884. A Toronto, Ontario-based company founded Toronto, U.K., as a mining town.

# CENTRE OF THE UNIVERSE

*"Toronto is kind of like New York run by the Swiss."*

—British actor and author Sir Peter Ustinov to the *Globe and Mail* in 1987

*"I've learned it's really run by the Canadians."*

—Ustinov again to the *Globe* in 1992

## Burp! What Province?

Sarcastically dubbed "the centre of the universe" and famously loathed by Canadians living outside its borders, Toronto is not a pretty city, nor as urbane and international as its leaders would like to believe. But as the fifth-biggest urban area in North America—after Mexico City, New York, Los Angeles and Chicago—it is hard to ignore. Despite their unpopularity, or perhaps in reaction to it, Torontonians are a fairly meek group, possessing a self-deprecating and ironic sense of humour.

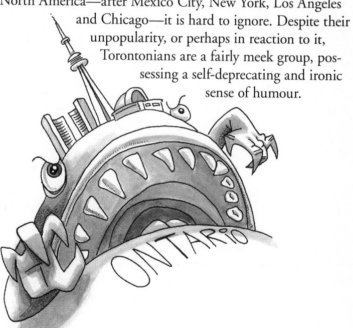

### Fancy a Drink?

When Toronto became a city in 1834, there was about one bar for every 120 people! By contrast, there was only one police constable for every 1850 citizens (and no police were on duty at night). Today, the ratio is one constable for every 475 citizens—one of the highest in North America. The ratio of bars to people today is unknown. But sadly for Torontonians, it's likely much lower than it used to be.

**DID YOU**  **KNOW?**

Toronto has the largest public library system in Canada, by number of branches (99), number of volumes (11 million) and number of patrons (2.3 million).

By contrast, the New York Public Library has only 85 branches (although Brooklyn and Queens have their own library systems, and there are 206 branches between the three of them).

## It's a Zoo

☞ The TorontoZoo is the largest zoo in Canada and one of the biggest in the world.
☞ It was built in 1974 and replaced the oldVictorian-style Riverdale Zoo.
☞ TheZoo is part of Rouge Park, the largest urban park in Canada.
☞ It includes 12,167 animals (made up of 476 species). Grrrr.

### No Longer Rolling Stoned

In 1979, Toronto police arrested Rolling Stones guitarist Keith Richards for heroin possession. A judge decided to punish Richards by forcing him to play an unbearably unhip concert—a benefit show for the blind in…Oshawa. Although they weren't required to, the rest of the band came along. Today, the Rolling Stones credit the experience for their renouncing of drugs, and now start many of their tours with free concerts in Toronto.

## John Paul II Superstar

World Youth Day—the international Catholic festival—was held in Toronto in 2002, and included a visit by then-Pope John Paul II. Nearly 500,000 Catholic teenagers from around the world visited Toronto, and about 800,000 people camped out to attend mass with the pope at the abandoned CFB Downsview airforce base. They occupied an area the size of 180 football fields, and the camp could have ranked as Canada's 10th largest city.

Supplies of 3 million hosts (wafers served with communion) and 752 litres of wine had to be obtained, 2000 priests and 500 archbishops, bishops and cardinals attended, and 3.5 million meals were served.

### DID YOU KNOW?

☞ Toronto has more people than Nova Scotia, Newfoundland, New Brunswick and Prince Edward Island combined.

☞ The city has less per capita representation politically than any other part of the country. A provincial riding in Prince Edward Island, for instance, has only 5000 voters, compared to almost 115,000 voters per riding in Toronto. Even city councillors in Toronto are supposed to represent 57,000 people each.

☞ On the other hand, Toronto is sometimes called the fifth-biggest government in Canada, after the federal government, Ontario, Québec and BC.

☞ Because—unlike prime ministers and premiers—the mayor of Toronto is elected directly by all its citizens, he or she receives more votes than any other politician in Canada.

Toronto was home to Canada's first vegetarian restaurant, opened by the Christian Women's Temperance Society in 1904.

# No Mistake About It...
# The World's Only Contraception Museum

One of Toronto's more unusual tourist attractions is the Contraception Museum, located in the Janssen-Ortho pharmaceutical company building. Some medieval contraceptive items in the collection include bones from the right side of a black cat, mule's earwax and dried weasel testicles. Apparently, mule's earwax is black. It was obtained for the museum—with considerable difficulty, no doubt—by employees of Janssen-Ortho's Mexican affiliate. Other hot tourist destinations in the city include the Police Services Museum, the Postal Museum, the Museum of Psychological Instruments and the Bata Shoe Museum.

### Val Kilmer Wasn't Here

For years, "Val Kilmer" has been far and away the most popular grafitti tag in Toronto, and photocopies of the American actor's face often appear pasted on bridges and abandoned buildings. Despite media scrutiny—from *Maclean's* and *People* magazine, amongst others—no explanation nor culprit has been found. Kilmer himself denies responsibility.

### Life's a Beach in Toronto

It may be hard for outsiders to believe that Toronto has any beaches suitable for swimming at all. In fact, it has 10, though they are often shut down because of pollution.

In 1999, Toronto got its first clothing-optional beach at Hanlan's Point (causing it to be nicknamed "Hanlan's Don't Point") on Toronto Islands. The achievement came as a result of arm twisting by the (likely powerful) nude lobby, which includes groups such as Totally Naked Toronto! Men Enjoying Nudity (or TNT!MEN). The area had a long-standing reputation for nudity, particularly with gay men.

In fact, in non-nude news, the beach is also home to an annual drag Queen Victoria lookalike contest on Victoria Day.

(Incidentally, the Federation of Canadian Naturists also recommends Beechgrove and Scarborough Bluffs beaches for covert skinny dipping, though they're not officially recognized.)

# It's Murder

Toronto has always had a bad reputation for crime and violence. More crimes occur in Toronto than any other city in the country—though statistics show that per capita, the crime rate in Toronto is lower in than most cities.

### 2004 MURDERS IN METROPOLITAN AREAS

| CITY | MURDERS | MURDERS PER 100,000 PEOPLE |
|------|---------|----------------------------|
| Regina | 10 | 4.98 |
| Winnipeg | 34 | 4.89 |
| Abbotsford | 7 | 4.39 |
| Edmonton | 34 | 3.39 |
| Saskatoon | 8 | 3.3 |
| Vancouver | 56 | 2.58 |
| Halifax | 9 | 2.37 |
| Calgary | 20 | 1.91 |
| Oshawa | 6 | 1.82 |
| **Toronto** | **94** | **1.8** |

# TAKING OUT
# THE TRASH

## It's a Dump

Most of the southern parts of downtown Toronto are built on "reclaimed" land—that is, space that was created by dumping old bricks, concrete and gravel into the lake and building over it. Fort York once stood on the edge of the water, and Front Street was once, as its name suggests, at the waterfront. The process is still happening, and several parks on artificial peninsulas have recently been created this way.

## It's Really a Dump

Much to the dismay of many Michigan residents and politicians, Toronto annually ships its one million tonnes of garbage to the Carlton Farms Landfill in that state. That's a whopping 125 truckloads per day. This began in 2001, after the city threw the last bag of trash into its Keele Valley Landfill site north of Toronto. The garbage export has so far continued—despite the protests of many people in Michigan.

### Where Does It Go?

The city's long-term waste plan calls for the elimination of all dumping by 2010. In 2002, Toronto introduced the Green Bin, a program in which the city picks up compostable waste. It is partly converted into compost and partly burned off as gas.

# GAY TORONTO

- Toronto has always been one of the main centres for Canada's queer community.
- Alexander Wood, a merchant and magistrate from Scotland, was banished in 1810 from Ontario after inspecting the genitals of several men—he claimed it was to gather information for a case he was investigating. Wood returned to Toronto in 1812. Alexander Street and Wood Street are named after him, where Toronto's gay village now stands. Wood has become a well-known martyr in the village, and a statue of him was recently put up.
- The first gay and lesbian student group was started at the University of Toronto in 1969—the year homosexuality was decriminalized in Canada. Known as the University of Toronto Homophile Association (UTHA), its first meeting drew only 16 people.
- In 1971, Toronto's first Gay Day Picnic was held at Hanlan's Point. The annual picnic would eventually become the Pride Parade, one of the largest events in Toronto and one of the largest queer events worldwide. It draws close to one million people annually.
- In 1972, Glad Day Books, Toronto's first gay bookstore, opened. In 1977, Buddies in Bad Times, the first gay theatre, was started.
- Bathhouse raids in 1980, 1981 and 2000 created conflict between the Toronto police and bathhouse customers.
- Bill Blair became the first police chief to participate in a Pride Parade in 2005.
- Toronto is home to the Canadian Lesbian and Gay Archives—one of the largest such institutions in the world.

# THE BETTER WAY

- Toronto has the third most used transit system in North America, after New York and Mexico City, though it is also the lowest funded. That may explain why you have your head in someone's armpit every morning.
- The Toronto Transit Commission (TTC) has 2.3 million riders daily, and claims to have moved the population of the world four times since its founding in 1921.
- Toronto is one of the only cities in North America to maintain its streetcar network, though many of the original streetcar lines have been dismantled.
- Toronto has the oldest subway system in Canada, with the first line opened in 1954.

☛ Unlike Montréal, which has deep subway stations, Toronto's stations tend to be small and close to the surface. That's because, unlike most cities where tunnelling was done to build subways, Toronto simply dug trenches to lay its original subways, and then covered them over. The city's subway station décor is also hardly up to Montréal's elaborate standards. It's frequently been described as "Stalinist"—though this is a bit of a misnomer, since Stalin himself actually was responsible for building some of the world's most exotic and decorative subway stations.

☛ One of the TTC's best-known legends is its abandoned Lower Bay subway station, located beneath Bay Station. The station was used for six months in 1966, and then shut down because the new Bloor-Danforth subway line had made it unnecessary. It is still fully operational and is used for movie shoots and training new drivers.

☛ Less known is that two other stations sit abandoned and incomplete: Allen Station, underneath Eglinton West Station, because of mid-1990s budget cuts that cancelled the Eglinton line; and Lower Queen Station, intended as part of a deep streetcar underpass in the 1940s—before the start of the subway system—that never happened.

☛ The nickname "Red Rocket" was originally applied ironically to Toronto's often slow, creaky streetcars. The name was officially adopted by the TTC in its promotional advertising in the 1980s. At typical rush-hour speed, about 10 kilometres per hour, a streetcar would take more than four years and four months to reach the moon.

# TORONTO NAMES AND NICKNAMES

*"But some people are moving out of Toronto, to Stratford or Kingston or Vancouver, squeezed out by housing prices or just fed up with frenzy and greed. What surprises me is how little regret they feel, the absence of any loyalty to Toronto. Perhaps it is because this city, unlike New York or Montréal, has created no myth of itself to hold them."*

—Cary Fagan, Toronto writer and literary journalist, 1990

## A Meeting Place or a Fish Trap in Orillia?

What would you like "Toronto" to mean? You've probably heard stories about where its name comes from—but chances are what you've heard is wrong.

City politicians like to believe that "Toronto" meant "meeting place" in the Huron language, suggesting something cosmopolitan or central. In fact, linguists agree that is a myth, going back to an error in a 19th century history book. "Toronto" likely comes from *tkoronto*, Huron for "where there are trees standing in water," and refers to a large weir, or fish trap, near Orillia. A popular trading route went between Orillia and modern-day Toronto, partly following the Humber River, which at one point became known as the Toronto River. When French traders built Fort Toronto, at the mouth of the Humber, the name stuck.

Fish Trap… Just doesn't have the same ring to it.

The city didn't officially go by the name "Toronto" until incorporation in 1834. Before that, it had been known as York, after Prince Frederick, Duke of York and son of King George III (Fredericton, New Brunswick, was also named after the Duke). Two earlier French outposts, once located around Toronto's Exhibition grounds and the Humber River, were known as Fort Rouillé and Fort Toronto. Previous to that, at least two fortified Seneca towns existed where Toronto does now: Ganatsekwyagon on the Rouge River and Teieiagon on the Humber.

Over the years, Toronto and its suburbs have gained a number of nicknames, few of them positive.

| Nickname | Origin |
| --- | --- |
| Hogtown | Named after the city's early proliferation of slaughterhouses. |
| T. O. or T-Dot | Short for Toronto, Ontario. |
| "La Ville Reine" | "The queen city." A Québecois nickname for Toronto, alluding to the city's supposed monarchism. |
| The Big Smoke | Obviously alluding to pollution and industrialism. A number of American cities are also nicknamed this. |
| Methodist Rome | A reference to the central role Toronto played for the Methodist religion. Most Methodist churches in Canada joined Presbyterians and Congregationalists to become the United Church. |
| Muddy York | An old nickname for Toronto, since it was supposedly one of the last North American cities to pave its streets. This, combined with Toronto's warm, slushy winters, seems like a fatal combination. |
| Toronto the Good | Alluding to the city's early reputation for conservative, religious behaviour. |
| Scarberia, Scarlem, Bramladesh, Flemmo… | Unpleasant nicknames for Toronto neighbourhoods, referencing Scarborough's supposed desolateness and high crime rate, Brampton's poverty and Flemingdon's, well, phlegminess… |

# FROM "METHODIST ROME" TO "THE MOST MULTICULTURAL CITY IN THE WORLD"

*"Irish beggars are to be met everywhere, and they are as ignorant and vicious as they are poor. They are lazy, improvident and unthankful; they fill our poorhouses and our prisons, and are as brutish in their superstition as Hindus."*

—Celebrated Reform leader George Brown, in a bigoted comment in the *Globe*, the paper he founded.

*"The only reason Toronto is no longer the dullest city on earth is that it is no longer full of Anglo-Canadians. It is full of Hong Kong Chinese. And not a few Italians."*

—Joel Garreau, Washington journalist, 1990

Toronto's old reputation as a bland, Anglo-Saxon city known for its conservative politics and conservative Protestantism is thankfully (at least mostly) dead.

DID YOU KNOW?

A huge oasis of green in Toronto's west end, High Park has traditionally been the main park in the city (though Rouge Park in Scarborough now dwarfs it). It was originally the private estate of architect John Howard, a gifted builder, but somewhat of a Victorian bigot. He donated it to the city on the conditions that the name of the park never be changed, that no alcohol ever be served there and that no Catholic ever be elected mayor of Toronto. The city has done its best to stay faithful on the first two points. The park was briefly renamed Howard Park, but changed back to High Park in keeping with Howard's wishes. Alcohol is still banned in the park, and it is not served in the one restaurant there. But there have now been several Catholic mayors of Toronto and—a fact that Howard probably never even considered—two Jewish mayors.

## Santa Claus Parade

At one time the biggest event of the year in Toronto—and still among the biggest—was the Santa Claus Parade. It started in 1905 and was originally named the Eaton's Santa Claus Parade (parades sponsored by Eaton's also occurred in Winnipeg and Montréal). Macy's Thanksgiving Parade in New York City is modelled after the Eaton's Santa Claus Parade.

### Queen's Birthday Parade
Members of the Monarchist League started the Queen's Birthday Parade in 1986, as the successor to the old Empire Day parades. It remains one of the few—perhaps the only—Victoria Day parades in Canada.

# The Most Multicultural?

Well, not really. A popular urban legend says that Toronto is "the most multicultural city in the world" and has been declared so by the United Nations. In the 1980s, the city's Multicultural Relations office put out a statement calling Toronto "one of the most multicultural cities in the world" and cited some UN statistics. That seems to have unleashed a broken-telephone series of misquotes and incorrect claims that continue to this day. Of course, there is no way to definitively measure a city's multiculturalism and the UN has never declared any city "the most multicultural in the world." However, a study released by the UN in 2004 comparing major cities did rank Toronto as having the second-highest percentage of foreign-born citizens in the world (after Miami, famous for is exiled Cuban population).

Toronto has the largest Portuguese and Greek populations in North America, and among the largest Chinese, Filipino, Jewish, South Asian, West Indian and Italian communities. Statistics show that Toronto is multicultural—at least by Canadian standards.

- ☛ 51 percent of Toronto's population was born outside of Canada (that's higher than any other major Canadian city).
- ☛ 48 percent have a mother tongue other than English.
- ☛ 43 percent of Toronto's citizens consider themselves to be visible minorities.
- ☛ 11 percent are Chinese.
- ☛ 10 percent are South Asian.
- ☛ 8 percent are Black.
- ☛ According to the 2001 census, Toronto's immigrants are mostly from China, India and Pakistan.

# ADOPTED TORONTONIANS

Over the years, Toronto has provided sanctuary or become a new home to dozens of international figures and Canadians from across the country.

- **Ernest Hemingway**, arguably the most famous American writer of all time, actually got his start as a journalist at the *Toronto Star*, between 1920 and 1924. He worked in Toronto and as a foreign correspondent in Europe, alongside fellow *Star* journalist and future author, Morley Callaghan.
- Singer and saxophonist **Tarig Abubakar**, one of Sudan's biggest stars, moved to Toronto in 1989 and became a leader in the city's African music scene. He died tragically in a car crash while visiting Sudan in 1998.
- **Colin Vaughan**, the late television journalist, started out as an architect in Australia and originally came to Toronto to work on the design of the Hummingbird Centre for the Performing Arts (originally called the O'Keefe Centre). His son Adam Vaughan now follows on his footsteps and is also a familiar face on CityTV newscasts.
- **Pier Giorgio di Cicco**, the celebrated poet (and Toronto's second poet laureate), moved to Toronto from Italy at a young age. Between 1986 and 2001, he gave up writing to become a priest, but returned to public life and published new work.
- Sri Lanka–born **Michael Ondaatje**, one of Canada's most famous authors, first came to Toronto at age 19. His brother, Christopher Ondaatje, also came and made a name for himself as an athlete, businessman and philanthropist.
- **Jane Jacobs**, famous American urban planner and author, settled in Toronto in 1969 to be with her draft-dodger son. Jacobs passed away in April 2006.

- **Ken Wiwa**, son of executed Nigerian environmentalist Ken Saro-Wiwa, works as a journalist and teaches at Massey College, an affiliate of the University of Toronto.
- **György Faludy**, Hungary's most famous poet of the 20th century, followed the path of many other Hungarians, making Toronto his home in 1967 after being exiled from his native land. In 1988, he returned to Hungary. A park dedicated to Faludy opened in Toronto in 2006.
- **David Miller,** the mayor in 2006, was actually born in San Francisco to an American father and an English mother. He moved to Toronto at age nine.
- Alberta-born **Marshall McLuhan**, famous media theorist who coined the phrase "global village," lived much of his life in Toronto, in the elite Wychwood neighbourhood.
- Famous feminist, labour agitator and anarchist **Emma Goldman** was born to a Jewish family in Lithuania, but made her name in turn-of-the-century Chicago politics. Exiled from the United States for her views, Goldman settled in Toronto's then Kensington Market area, where she became a major political figure. She died in 1940 and was buried in Chicago near the Haymarket Martyrs' Monument, alongside other famous American labour leaders.
- Born in 1952 in Bombay (now Mumbai), India, **Rohinton Mistry**, the author of *A Fine Balance* and *Such a Long Journey,* originally wrote in his free time while working in a bank in Brampton.
- An accidental Torontonian, NDP leader **Jack Layton** was born in Hudson, Québec, to a wealthy family with a long history in politics. His father was a Conservative cabinet minister, his grandfather was in the Québec cabinet and his great-great uncle was a Father of Confederation. He came to Toronto to attend York University. **Olivia Chow**, Layton's wife and fellow MP, was born in Hong Kong. She came to Toronto as a child.
- German immigrant and artist **Gustav Hahn** is best known for his massive murals painted in the 1890s on the ceiling

of the Legislative Building in Queen's Park. They were recently rediscovered after being whitewashed over.

☞ Jamaican-born Olympic gold medal–winning track star **Donovan Bailey** arrived in Canada with his family at age 13, settling in Oakville. Disgraced runner Ben Johnson was also a Jamaican immigrant.

☞ Although unknown outside of Toronto, just about anyone living in the downtown area of the city is familiar with film archivist **Reg Hartt**, or at least his name—it appears on posters, which cover almost every inch of many walls and telephone poles. Originally from New Brunswick, Hartt has held public screenings of obscure and historic movies in his living room for years (including the "Anarchist Surrealist Hallucinatory Film Festival" and the the "Sex and Violence Cartoon Festival").

☞ Another eccentric Maritimer to make Toronto his home was the late **Ben Kerr**—busker, would-be politician and cayenne pepper enthusiast. Kerr was born in Yarmouth, Nova Scotia, and came to Toronto to perform in then hippie-populated Yorkville as a folksinger. He became increasingly obsessed with cayenne pepper, which he credited with improving his health. He wrote the book *The Cayenne Pepper Cocktail Does It All* and frequently appeared on MuchMusic to emit sound bites such as: "Everything's better with cayenne pepper." Kerr ran for mayor of Toronto in every election from 1985 to 2000 (always losing by a wide margin) and was a fixture at the corner of Bloor and Yonge, singing country music with a karaoke machine.

☞ The artist formerly known as the Artist Formerly Known as **Prince** owns a house in Toronto, where he lives part-time. His wife, Manuela Testolini, is from Toronto.

# FAMOUS RIOTS AND UPRISINGS

*"Loyalty to the queen does not require a man to bow down to her manservant, her maidservant or her ass."*
—Prime Minister Alexander Mackenzie

*William Lyon Mackenzie,*
*Came to town in a frenzy,*
*Shot off his gun and made himself run,*
*William Lyon Mackenzie."*
—Limerick by Dennis Lee, former Toronto poet laureate

"Peace, order and good government" was a description of the Canadian ideal, as written by Lord Durham in his report on how to reform Canadian politics, following the 1837 Rebellions in Ontario and Québec. Well, sometimes it's been anything but.

### 1837

The 1837 Rebellion is the largest armed insurrection since the founding of Ontario. Some 500 rebels gathered at Montgomery's Tavern, near the intersection of modern-day Lawrence Avenue and Yonge Street (No doubt hosting the meeting seemed like a good business decision for the pub's owner, since it required a good deal of alcohol to fortify their spirits. However, it got his establishment burned down in the end.)

The group was defeated on the way down to Toronto in the Battle of Yonge Street and then finally finished off (back at the pub) at the Battle of Montgomery's Tavern. The rebels criticized the colonial government for being undemocratic and run by a small clique. William Lyon Mackenzie, leader of the rebels, escaped to Navy Island in the Niagara River and later to the United States. A second pincer of the rebellion, rallying under Dr. Charles Duncombe near Brantford, heard about Mackenzie's failure, got the willies and fled. Rebel groups in the U.S. made several unsuccessful invasion attempts, most famously the Battle of the Windmill. That involved a small landing near Kingston, led by Swedish mercenary Nils von Schoultz. The group was cornered and decided to hole up in a stone windmill. They surrendered after several days, having used up their ammunition, which included their buttons and belt buckles.

# Orangemen

Members of the Orange Order—a Protestant, pro-British Irish fraternity—featured heavily in 19th-century Toronto street fighting, as they do in Northern Ireland today. Some of the most famous Orange riots are noted below.

### MONRO RIOTS

In 1841, Orangemen supporters of Toronto mayor George Monro rioted when he lost in a bid to be elected to Parliament. They attacked the winning candidate's victory parade and shot dead one marcher. Charles Dickens, during his visit to Toronto in 1842, criticized the riot and the city's "rabid Toryism" that fuelled it.

### ST. PATRICK'S DAY RIOTS

In 1858, members of the Orange Order attacked a St. Patrick's Day parade, killing one marcher. The situation repeated itself in the Jubilee Riots of 1875. Irish sectarian violence was to be a major factor in Ontario politics until the early 20th century, and conflicts often turned violent. Orangemen parades were also frequent causes of violence, especially when they passed through Catholic neighbourhoods.

### THE FIREMAN'S RIOT AND THE CIRCUS RIOT

On June 29, 1855, two rival volunteer fire departments tried to put out a fire and began fighting with each other instead. Police tried to break them up and eventually charged a number of firefighters with assault. On July 13, a second riot started when clowns from a travelling circus got into a brawl with local Orange Order–affiliated firemen at a brothel. Firemen went on to tear down the show tent and set circus wagons on fire. The police (sympathetic to the Orangemen) refused to intervene, and the riot only ended after the mayor called in the army.

Besides the Orange Order violence, there have been other riots.

### Christie Pits Race Riot

In 1933, when the Nazi Party and swastika clubs were popular in Toronto, a baseball game at Christie Pits Park between a Jewish team and an Anglo team turned violent. A local gang displayed a swastika flag and a "Heil Hitler" sign. Thousands of youths raged a five-hour battle until the flag was torn down and ripped up.

### The Yonge Street Riot

In May 1992, following the infamous Los Angeles Riots, rioting also broke out in Toronto and many stores along the city's main street were damaged.

### The Queen's Park Riot

On June 15, 2000, several thousand people marched with the Ontario Coalition Against Poverty (OCAP) to Queen's Park to protest poverty and lack of affordable housing in Toronto. The result was a violent clash that saw dozens of protestors beaten and arrested. A number of police and their horses were injured. The protestors called it a "police riot"—initiated by the cops—and after a mistrial, the charges against OCAP organizer John Clarke were dropped.

# WAR

## X Marks the Spot

Never heard of Camp X? Well, you weren't supposed to. Probably the most secret military base in Canadian history, Camp X was located between Whitby and Oshawa. It was opened in 1941 by the Canadian government and the British Secret Intelligence Service. In addition to training British and Canadian agents, it secretly taught Americans in espionage, before the United States' official entry into the Second World War. Many early OSS (Office of Strategic Services, predecessor to the CIA) agents got their start at Camp X, as did Sir Ian Fleming, the British secret agent who would later become famous for his James Bond novels. Now you know. Once you've finished reading this trivia book, eat it.

# Ontario, New Ireland?

The last military engagement in Ontario happened in 1866, when a group of 500 armed Fenians crossed the Niagara River. (Fenians were Irish nationalists who supported an armed overthrow of the British authorities in Ireland. Because of their politics, and the general economic situation in Ireland, many wound up in the United States. Some gained fighting experience by participating in the American Civil War.) They hoped to capture control of Canada, rename it New Ireland and hold it hostage to Britain until the original Ireland was liberated. They only got as far as Ridgeway, near Fort Erie, where despite winning a battle against the Canadian militia, they soon withdrew to the U.S., fearing that more British troops were on their way.

**DID YOU**  **KNOW?**

Canada's first Victoria Cross recipient, Alexander Robert Dunn of Toronto, won the award for his role in the Battle of Balaclava in 1854 in the Crimean War. Modern day thieves also have reason to remember the fight—because during the battle, British troops invented the wool ski mask, or balaclava.

 The greatest flying ace ever produced in Canada or the Commonwealth was Owen Sound's Billy Bishop. Bishop was credited with 72 kills during the First World War. He was awarded the Victoria Cross for shooting down three German planes in one flight (though it is often said that he exaggerated his description of the attack). Bishop was later promoted to Honorary Air Marshal and put in charge of recruiting for the massive air force training program during the Second World War.

Less well remembered is Roy Brown of Carleton Place. Brown was officially credited with shooting down and killing Manfred von Richthofen—better known as the "Red Baron," Germany's most famous ace. Most historians now agree that it was probably Australian soldiers on the ground, not Brown, who killed the Red Baron.

# 100,000 Tulips

During the Second World War, many Europeans sought refuge in Canada. Among them was Princess Juliana of the Netherlands, who would later become queen. She gave birth to her daughter Margriet in Ottawa Civic Hospital—which was temporarily declared Dutch territory. Canadian forces later liberated the Netherlands, and the relationship between the Netherlands and Canada has since always been strong. In 1945, Juliana had 100,000 tulip bulbs sent to Ottawa, and 20,000 have been sent every year since.

**What War?**
Although mostly forgotten, almost 1500 Canadians fought in the Spanish Civil War between 1937 and 1938, in an unsuccessful attempt to block the fascist military takeover of Spain. Half of them died. The group, called the Mackenzie-Papineau Battalion, after the leaders of the 1837 Rebellions, met and organized the expedition in Toronto, from their offices at the corner of Queen and Spadina.

**DID YOU  KNOW?**

Call it the "Diefenblunder." Whereas most Canadians had to be content with ducking and covering, federal bureaucrats and politicians, as well as military leaders, had more elaborate plans for their own protection during the Cold War. A number of "Diefenbunkers"—underground concrete bunkers designed to

withstand nuclear attacks—were built, the largest at Carp, near Ottawa. It's now a museum of Cold War history, featuring bland 1960s-era government offices, an emergency CBC broadcast centre and a tiny—but charmingly radiation-free—prime ministerial bedroom with a twin-size bed.

Opposition politicians sarcastically coined the name "Diefenbunker," in reference to Prime Minister John Diefenbaker, who ordered the bunkers.

# CRIME

## Um...No Thanks

Early Toronto had trouble finding police officers to patrol its streets. The province took to ordering citizens to become constables, press gang style. Several residents were fined considerable amounts for refusing to serve as police officers.

### A Cop in Every Inn

Crime was so widespread in 19th-century Ontario that the government declared that every innkeeper would have to act as a constable. This law stayed in place from 1823 to as late as 1887.

As of 1996, following a legal battle by the intrepid toplessness activist Gwen Jacob of Guelph, it is no longer a crime for women to bare their breasts in public in Ontario.

### A Lawyer with Experience

The last recorded duel in Ontario happened on June 13, 1833, near Perth (today, the pistols used are on display in the Perth Museum). Two friends, John Wilson and Robert Lyon, fought over a woman, Elizabeth Hughes. Lyon was killed, and Wilson was acquitted for murder. He later married Hughes and became a criminal defence lawyer.

DID YOU KNOW?

Toronto's infamous Don Jail, completed in 1865, was the site of Canada's last executions in 1962. On December 11 of that year, Ronald Turpin and Arthur Lucas were hanged after being convicted of murder. The jail, used mainly as a short-term lockup, has had a bad reputation for overcrowding and violence.

# Ellis, the Executioners

Canada's last executions were arranged by John Ellis, one of a long line of Ellises to work as hangmen. In 1976, he appeared on CBC television to defend the death penalty, wearing a black hood over his head to protect his identity. Ellis remained on the government payroll until 1980, though he was living in Barbados at the time. Arthur English—who used the pseudonym "Arthur Ellis"—had previously worked as Canada's official executioner. Some of his work had even more gruesome-than-expected results. Twice, a mistake in getting a prisoner's weight right led to the person's head coming off during the hanging. Arthur was related to another John Ellis, who was one of Britain's official executioners, and who came from a family that had been involved with carrying out hangings for some 300 years.

### Gallows Humour?

The darkly named Arthur Ellis Awards are given out today to reward crime and mystery writing in Canada.

DID YOU KNOW?

American-born Harry Oakes came to Kirkland Lake in northern Ontario in 1911 and made a fortune in gold prospecting. He was later knighted for his philanthropy, and established two massive houses, in Kirkland Lake and Niagara Falls. By 1920, he was the richest man in Canada and owner of the second-richest gold mine in North America. In order to escape income taxes—in the best tradition of many wealthy Canadians—he left Canada and moved to the Bahamas. In 1943, he was found murdered in his bed. His son-in-law was accused of the crime but was later acquitted, leaving the mystery of Oakes' death unsolved.

## The Boyd Gang

Named after their leader, Edwin Alonzo Boyd, the Boyd Gang terrorized Toronto with sensational bank robberies in the 1940s and 1950s. Police caught up with the gang in 1952. Two of its members were hanged for the murder of a police detective. Boyd himself was paroled in 1966, changed his name and moved to British Columbia, where he died in 2002. After his death, his therapist made public tapes in which Boyd confessed to killing—just for practice—two lovers he had randomly stumbled onto in 1947. That crime would have been enough to hang him in 1952.

# Sam Steele

Could he have asked for a better name? Canada's most famous Mountie was born in Orillia in 1849. Samuel Benfield Steele, a career soldier, was hired to lead the North West Mounted Police (later to become the RCMP) in the Yukon during a gold rush. He is famous for bringing order to an amazingly chaotic event and announcing that anyone entering the Yukon had to bring with them a ton of supplies. Steele popularized the image of the RCMP as a highly organized, tough and fair police force. Mount Steele in the Yukon is named after him.

ONLY IN ONTARIO

In Canada, only Ontario, Québec and Newfoundland have provincial police forces. The Ontario Provincial Police, or OPP, was founded in 1909 to maintain order in northern mining towns and started with only 45 men. The force now numbers more than 5000 officers (plus more than 2000 other staff) and is based in Orillia. On the cover of the Beatles' album *Sargeant Pepp 'Lonely Hearts Club Band*, Paul McCartney is wearing

# PRISONS

**Made in Ontario**

Possibly Canada's best known jail, Kingston Penitentiary (maximum security) is also one of the world's oldest. It was built as the Provincial Penitentiary of the Province of Upper Canada in 1835 and was Canada's first jail with a mission to rehabilitate rather than simply punish inmates. From 1835 to 1934, women prisoners were also housed in a wing of the penitentiary.

☛ Inmates in Kingston Pen sewed the original uniforms used by the North West Mounted Police. They were also responsible for forging some of the metalwork used in the parliamentary library in Ottawa.

☛ Ever wonder what people did before gangster movies? In the 19th century, the jail attracted tourists and even charged them admission.

☛ The first inmate in the Kingston Pen was Joseph Bouchette of Northumberland County. He was sentenced to five years for grand larceny on January 14, 1835.

☛ In 1878, a nine-year-old girl was sentenced to seven years in the prison for housebreaking and larceny. She was found guilty of stealing a quilt, a hat, a towel, a jug, beef, raisins, sugar, tea and biscuits.

☛ The prison's youngest inmate was Antoine Beauche, age eight, of Québec City. He was sentenced to three years for pickpocketing. The boy was whipped 47 times in his first nine months in prison for savage offences such as staring, laughing, whistling and idling.

☛ At least 50 people have successfully escaped from the prison in 26 jailbreaks, the first in 1836. The latest person to do it was Ty Conn, who scaled the wall in 1999. He made it to Toronto, but died after shooting himself during a media interview, possibly by accident.

☛ There are eight other jails in the Kingston area, including Millhaven Institution (also maximum security). A large prison break from Millhaven in 1973, involving 12 escapees, inspired the Tragically Hip song "38 Years Old."

## Celebrity Budget Inn

It doesn't sound like a holiday. Until it was replaced in 2004, Toronto's secretive immigrant detention centre was concealed in the back of the Celebrity Budget Inn, a functioning motel near the airport.

## Battle of Bowmanville

The majority of Canada's Second World War POW camps for captured German and Italian soldiers were in Ontario. Reports say that Canadian military prisons were among the most comfortable in the world, however they were not without conflicts. A three-day riot, nicknamed the Battle of Bowmanville, broke out when German officers in the camp were shackled in retribution for Canadian POWs captured in the Battle of Dieppe being treated in a similar way. One German POW was killed and a number of prison guards were injured.

DID YOU KNOW?

German Luftwaffe officer Franz von Werra was the only one of over 30,000 Second World War POWs to successfully escape from Canada and return home. He jumped off a train carrying prisoners as it passed near Smith's Falls and managed to make it through the woods to Prescott, where he stole a rowboat and crossed the partially frozen St. Lawrence to get to the U.S. Because the U.S. was still neutral in 1941, he was not immediately returned to Canada. With the help of the German consulate in New York City, he was smuggled across the Mexican border and then back to Germany.

None of this ultimately proved helpful to von Werra, since he disappeared during a flight shortly after returning to duty.

## The Great Escape

Twenty-eight German prisoners escaped from a POW camp in Angler, near Marathon, on April 18, 1942, by digging a 60-metre-long tunnel. All of them were recaptured, though some got as far as Medicine Hat, Alberta.

# TAXING TIMES

*"The promises of yesterday are the taxes of today."*
—Prime Minister William Lyon Mackenzie King

*"Hello, Mr. Wilson"*
—U.S. President Lyndon B. Johnson to Prime Minister Lester Pearson

*"You will never be mayor of this city…because you say stupid and dumb things!"*
—then Toronto mayor Mel Lastman to David Miller, who would replace him

## Prime Ministers

Five prime ministers have been born in Ontario: Arthur Meighen, William Lyon Mackenzie King, John Diefenbaker, Lester B. Pearson and Paul Martin. Sir John A. Macdonald and Alexander Mackenzie lived in Ontario but were born in Scotland. Likewise, Sir Mackenzie Bowell and John Turner lived in Ontario but were born in England.

Toronto has not yet given birth to a prime minister (though King and Alexander Mackenzie at times represented ridings in Toronto).

## Premiers

Although he is scarcely known, Ontario's first premier was John Sanfield Macdonald, from St. Raphael, near Ottawa. He was a distant relative of the much more famous John Alexander Macdonald, the first prime minister of Canada. Ontario premiers were originally called prime ministers.

### Pint-Sized Politicos

Could it be a Napoleanic syndrome? Ontario's capital city has had a number of eccentric—and short—politicians.

In 1834, Toronto's first mayor, William Lyon Mackenzie, was known for his small stature, hot temper and radical politics (as well as his bright red wig) and earned the nickname the "Little Rebel." Fondly remembered David Crombie, who headed the city during the 1980s, was known as "the tiny perfect mayor." The first mayor of amalgamated Toronto, in which the six cities of Metropolitan Toronto were merged, was Mel Lastman. Standing 5'5" and called "the tiny Tory," Lastman was responsible for dozens of foot-in-the-mouth gaffes.

## Pell Mel

Toronto's most successful and most mocked politician, Mel Lastman, was mayor of North York from 1972 to 1997 and mayor of Toronto from 1998 to 2003. He won 80 percent of the vote in 2000 (albeit with a very low voter turnout). Lastman started off as an appliance salesman, founding Bad Boy Furniture, a company that became known for bizarre publicity stunts. Even after selling the company and becoming mayor of North York, Lastman frequently appeared on Bad Boy ads, shouting what became his catchphrase: "Who's better for furniture? Nooobody!!" When he employed a Bill Clinton impersonator on the ads, Lastman received a letter from the American president's lawyers telling him to stop. He refused and later added a Hillary Clinton impersonator to the commercials.

As mayor of Toronto, Lastman is remembered for spending some $200,000 on giant fibreglass moose placed around the city, hoping to build a Canadian theme to promote tourism. Most of the statues were vandalized by aggressive urban moose hunters and were quickly removed. One radio show offered free concert tickets to listeners who turned in a pair of severed fibreglass antlers.

In a more serious matter, Lastman eventually grudgingly acknowledged that he had a long-term affair with Grace Louie, a former Bad Boy employee. However, he successfully fought off a lawsuit for support payments by her sons Todd and Kim Louie.

Although his goofiness was endearing to many, Torontonians eventually seemed to tire of Lastman's awful slipups. With support dropping in the polls and his health declining, Lastman decided to retire rather than run for mayor again.

No one can say that Lastman didn't apologize for his mistakes—he often seemed to be constantly and tearfully saying that he was sorry.

Here are some of Lastman's most famous offensive slipups:

- Saying, "What the hell do I want to go to a place like Mombasa? I just see myself in a pot of boiling water with all these natives dancing around me," when describing his trip to Kenya to promote one of Toronto's several failed Olympic bids. Critics accused him of racism.
- Threatening to kill a TV journalist who reported that his wife was charged with shoplifting for stealing a pair of gloves from Eaton's.
- Shaking hands with members of the Hells Angels and accepting a T-shirt from them. The next day, in front of reporters, he apologized and dramatically threw the T-shirt into the garbage.
- Claiming that homelessness didn't exist in North York, only to have a homeless woman freeze to death in Mel Lastman Square (the plaza beside the former North York City Hall that Lastman had named after himself) shortly after.
- Following what could be described as a slightly worse than usual snowfall, Lastman ordered in the military to help shovel snow. This slipup is mostly forgotten in Toronto, but may make Lastman a household name for generations in other, colder parts of Canada.

DID YOU KNOW?

Nineteenth-century reform politician Robert Baldwin was a sentimental, sometimes downright weird guy. When his wife died during childbirth after a failed caesarean section, Baldwin blamed himself and fell into a deep depression that lasted most of his remaining years. When he died 10 years later, he asked that his coffin be chained to his wife's and that their love letters be placed in each other's coffins. Finally, he asked that an incision be made in his body that approximated a caesarean. Baldwin's daughter fulfilled the first two requests, but balked at the third. A few days after the burial, feeling guilty, his son had his father dug up and the incision made.

# The Biggest Loser

John C. Turmel of Ottawa is proud to be the biggest political loser the world has ever seen. He has lost 61 elections so far, since 1979—federal, provincial and municipal, in various parts of Ontario, Québec and Nova Scotia—and is listed in the *Guinness Book of World Records*. Turmel's platform—likely a reason why he never gets elected—includes a mixture of old Social Credit monetary policies, conspiracy theory, support for legalizing gambling and marijuana, and fringe Christian theology that involves seeing Christ mainly as a monetary reformist. He founded three unsuccessful parties—the Christian Credit Party, the Social Credit Party of Ontario (unconnected to other Social Credit parties) and the Abolitionist Party. He was expelled from the federal Socred party and the Green Party. He has frequently been in trouble with the law for trying to run illegal gambling dens—the largest of which, "Casino Turmel," had 28 tables. Turmel's trademark is his white construction helmet. He is often seen playing the accordion at public events.

## Assassinations

Thomas D'Arcy McGee was shot dead in Ottawa in 1868, one of only two political assassinations in Canadian history (Pierre Laporte, killed during the 1970 October Crisis, was the other). McGee—one of the Fathers of Confederation—was likely killed by an Irish nationalist, upset over McGee's support for Britain. Patrick James Whalen, a member of the radical Fenian Brotherhood, was hanged for McGee's murder, but many people continue to believe he was framed. He was the last person to be publicly executed in Canada.

(Eight aboriginal men were publicly hanged in 1885 in what was to become Saskatchewan, but was not technically part of Canada at the time).

People say Whalen's ghost haunts the old jail he was kept in before his execution, which is now a travellers' hostel. Guests have reported seeing a ghost figure leave a cell and walk down the hall, murmuring the Lord's Prayer—supposedly Whalen's last words.

## A Miscalculation

In 1917, Premier Howard Hearst gave women the vote (at least, those over the age of 21). It may not have been the best decision for Hearst—he lost the next provincial election, in 1919.

### A Good Time, Not a Long Time

Ontario's shortest-serving Premier was Frank Miller, who stayed in office for only three months in 1985.

DID YOU KNOW?

Canada's first Canadian-born Governor General was Vincent Massey, the appropriately aristocratic heir to the massive Massey-Ferguson Tractor Company fortune. Serving as Governor General 1952 to 1959, Massey was well known for his philanthropy. After briefly serving as a cabinet minister in Mackenzie King's government, he went on to become the first Canadian ambassador to the United States in 1926 (before that, Canada's foreign policy was technically set by Britain). Massey later became High Commissioner to the U.K.

## Parliament, Take Two

Canada's first national Parliament buildings almost completely burned down in 1916. The parliamentary library was the only part saved—thanks to the heavy metal doors separating it from the rest of the building. The current Parliament was built in 1919, featuring a stone interior (mindful of the wood panelling that burned so quickly in the last structure!) and the characteristic 92-metre-tall Peace Tower, commemorating the end of the First World War. Until the 1970s, a city bylaw said that no other building in the city could be taller than 45.7 metres. Today, there are seven buildings in Ottawa taller than the Peace Tower.

# ECOLOGICAL GAFFS

*And the blackflies, the little blackflies,*
*Always the blackfly no matter where you go,*
*I'll die with the blackfly a pickin' my bones*
*In north Ontar-i-o-i-o, in north Ontar-i-o*
—"The Blackfly Song" by Wade Hemsworth

## Macoun's Shining Moss

Ontario's only known extinct plant is Macoun's shining moss, which existed in one swamp near Belleville. Samples collected by naturalist John Macoun in the early 19th century are the only evidence of its existence. The swamp was cleared out between 1862 and 1892.

DID YOU  KNOW?

A moraine is a chain of small hills formed by ice-age glaciers. Among southern Ontario's best-known geographic features is the 200-kilometre Oak Ridges Moraine, stretching from Peterborough to beyond Orangeville.

 The province's first park, Algonquin, was set up in 1893. However, it has no old-growth forest, having been thoroughly logged before becoming a park.

## The Air of Our Ways

In 2000, 1900 Ontarians died from pollution-related illnesses. Also that year, pollution caused 13,000 emergency room visits and 47 million minor illnesses.

## Tire Fire

The Hagersville tire fire—one of the worst environmental disasters in Ontario's history—lasted for 17 days in 1990. Twelve million used tires burned after teenagers set a fire.

# WILD ONTARIO

## Vampires of the Great Lakes

The sea lamprey first showed up in Lake Ontario in 1835, brought by ships from the Atlantic. It squirmed its way to Lake Erie in 1921, then to Lake Huron in 1932, Lake Michigan in 1936 and Lake Superior in 1946. An eel-like parasite, something straight out of a nightmare, it clings with its teeth to the side of fish and gradually sucks the fish's blood until the host dies. It has devastated the lakes' fish populations.

Perhaps even more harmful, to humans at least, is the zebra mussel, an Asian shellfish that reproduces rapidly and blocks drinking and irrigation pipes.

**Butterflies**

The Niagara Butterfly Conservatory, opened in 1996, has more than 2000 butterflies in its tropical greenhouses. Visitors walk through flocks of butterflies.

# Death Rattle of Extinction

Ontario may or may not have more than one poisonous snake. The timber rattlesnake is considered to be highly endangered, and there has not been a confirmed sighting since the 1940s. More common, but considered threatened, is the eastern massassauga rattlesnake, found mostly on the Bruce Peninsula or on the eastern side of Georgian Bay. In either case, watch your step.

 Winnie the Pooh is an Ontarian. A.A. Milne named his famous character after his son Christopher Robin's toy bear, which in turn was named after a real female bear at the London Zoo named Winnipeg. "Winnie" had come to the U.K. as the mascot of a cavalry unit from Manitoba. They bought her for $20 from a trapper they met on the railway platform in White River, Ontario, on their way to France during the First World War.

 DID YOU KNOW?

One of Ontario's strangest wild animals is the Virginia opossum. Opossums are the only North American marsupial (that is, mammals that carry their young in a pouch, like their better known Aussie relatives, the kangaroo and the koala). Opossums (the "o" is silent) are best known for "playing dead" when threatened. Their muscles contract and they fall into a coma-like state that can last a few hours, hinting to predators that they might not be safe to eat.

The species has been moving up from the southern United States over the past century and began showing up in Ontario a few decades ago. Some people have theorized that the opossums crossed the frozen Niagara River during the winter, whereas others suggest that they may have clung onto trucks or trains crossing the border. Despite being badly suited for cold weather—they are partly hairless—opossums are now found all over the province, including in urban areas.

# HOW WAS WORK?

## The First Labour Day

Quick, check the calendar. Now, check your clothes. Are you wearing white?

The Labour Day holiday celebrated in Canada and the U.S. (and in Australia, though at a different time of year) started in Ontario.

☛ It began with a parade on April 15, 1872, in Toronto, organized by the Toronto Trades Assembly. On September 3 of that year, unions in Ottawa followed it up with a parade in the capital, this one featuring Sir John A. Macdonald. Although not exactly a friend of labour, the shrewd politician was able to win working man support to defeat the Liberals.

☛ On the 10th anniversary of the marches, in 1882, labour unions held another parade in Toronto. American workers invited to the parade liked the idea so much that they launched the tradition at home.

☛ Toronto still has an annual Labour Day march, held on the last day of the Canadian National Exhibition (CNE). Union members march through the Dufferin Gates and get free entrance to the CNE. It is traditional for unscrupulous thrill-seekers to blend into the parade to avoid paying the ticket price.

### The Auto Industry

The biggest industry in Ontario and still the core of the province's economy is the automobile industry. In fact, all of Canada's auto plants are in Ontario.

☛ One out of every six vehicles built in North America is produced in Ontario.

- There are 48,000 autoworkers in Ontario working in 14 plants—plus another 90,000 in over 400 auto parts factories. One in every six jobs in Ontario is tied directly or indirectly to the auto industry.
- About 2.7 million cars roll out of Ontario plants every year—more than 80 percent for export to the U.S. The car and auto parts industries in the province together sell $95 billion worth of products annually.
- Ontario produces more cars than any American state—including Michigan, usually thought to be the centre of the industry.
- The average wage of a worker at General Motors plant in Windsor is $51.05 per hour.

# FAMOUS BUSINESSES

*Honest Ed doesn't want to achieve immortality through his work.*
*He wants to achieve it by not dying.*
—Honest Ed's Slogan

## McLaughlin Motors
It all started with the McLaughlin Carriage Company, which
was producing 25,000 carriages a year from its Oshawa plant
in 1901. In 1907, McLaughlin began building cars and later
merged with Buick. The brand was known as McLaughlin,
and then McLaughlin-Buick and eventually just Buick. In
1918, it was sold to General Motors. Oshawa has remained one
of Ontario's car building cities—along with Windsor, Oakville,
Brampton, Woodstock, Cambridge, Ingersoll and Alliston.

## Hudson's Bay Company
Probably Canada's oldest and most famous business, the Bay,
started out in 1670 as a royally chartered fur-trading outfit.
It established the first English settlement in Ontario—Moose
Factory—on James Bay, largely thanks to two French *coureurs
de bois* who had their application for a fur-trading license
turned down by authorities in New France. Generations of
English-speaking schoolchildren have nicknamed Pierre-
Ésprit Radisson and Médard de Groseilliers as "Radishes"
and "Gooseberries." In 1989, the Bay finally abandoned its
last stakes in the fur industry. Early in 2006, the remaining
retailing icon was bought by an American investor.

## T. Eaton Company Ltd.
Irish immigrant Timothy Eaton started Eaton's in 1869 in
the small town of St. Mary's, Ontario. Eaton opened a store
in Toronto shortly afterwards, and it became a major success.
At one time, it was Canada's biggest retailer. Within 25 years,

Eaton's was calling itself "Canada's greatest store" and had come to dominate the department store and mail-order catalogue business. It later expanded into Manitoba and Québec, and then across the country. In 1977, the massive nine-storey Eaton's Centre, the largest shopping centre in downtown Toronto, opened, replacing two locations. But Eaton's couldn't keep it up and went bankrupt in 1999, selling its stores to American chain Sears.

Despite Eaton's ultimate failure, the giant seated statue of Timothy Eaton, which once graced the lobby of the central store in Toronto, is still venerated by aspiring business people. It is now in the Royal Ontario Museum, and it is said to be good luck to rub his (well-worn) toe. Other Eaton's memorabilia is on display in the Eaton's Museum in St. Mary's. Old Timothy may not have been a saint, but he was good enough to be one of the few non-saints to have a church named after him. Timothy Eaton Memorial Church is located in midtown Toronto.

## CANADIAN TIRE CORPORATION LTD.

Brothers J.W. and A.J. Billes opened Canadian Tire in Toronto in 1922, at the corner of Yonge and Davenport. The façade of the original store remains, and Canadian Tire is now one of the nation's biggest chains, with more than 430 stores and 200 gas stations. The company claims that 90 percent of adult Canadians shop at Canadian Tire at least twice a year.

Canadian Tire money, probably Canada's most successful customer reward program, has nearly become a national icon.

☞ That's despite that company has become less generous with the program—at times in the past, Canadian Tire money was given out at the rate of five percent of a customer's purchase, but now sits at 1.5 percent.

- The colourful currency was introduced in 1958 and there have been 21 different designs to date—enough to create a mini-industry of Canadian Tire money collectors.
- Canadian Tire money was originally printed on actual banknote paper by the British-American Banknote Company, which was also contracted by the federal government to print money.
- The mysterious man pictured on the money, in Scottish costume, is the fictional Sandy McTire.
- Unsuspecting Americans have often had Canadian Tire money passed off on them as actual currency.
- In a bizarre case in 2001, Canadian Tire tried to prevent the Internet domain name www.crappytire.com from being registered. Apparently Canadian Tire had trademarked the name "crappy tire," and in its legal submissions admitted that many Canadians refer to the chain as "Crappy Tire."

## Leon's Furniture Ltd.

Lebanese immigrant Ablan Leon started furniture chain Leon's, one of the first companies to use huge warehouse-style stores, in 1909 in Welland.

## Sam the Record Man

Sam Sniderman opened Sam the Record Man, a Toronto icon known for its giant flashing neon signs on Yonge Street, in 1936 as a section inside his parents' radio store. In 2001, the chain went bankrupt and most of its stores closed. The flagship Toronto store remains open, owned by Sniderman's sons.

## Mr. Christie's

In the late 19th century, Scottish immigrant William Mellis Christie and partners launched the giant cookie manufacturer in Toronto. The company later became famous for the slogan: "Mr. Christie, you make good cookies." Although Nabisco now owns it, the company still has a factory in Toronto. Christie Street is named after it.

## Honest Ed's

American immigrant Ed Mirvish started Honest Ed's, Toronto's characteristic flashy, trashy, light-covered discount store in 1948. Mirvish covered the building with phrases such as: "Honest Ed's a freak: he has bargains coming out of his ears!" and "Squirrels love Honest Ed. They think he's nuts!" Mirvish became known for flamboyant stunts, including riding an elephant. He later bought the Royal Alexandra Theatre and opened the Princess of Wales Theatre. The area around Honest Ed's became known as Mirvish Village. Mirvish once ran several blocks of generic restaurants—with names such as Most Honourable Ed's Chinese Restaurant, Ed's Italian and Ed's Seafood—on King Street His first restaurant, Ed's Warehouse, sold only one meal: roast beef, mashed potatoes, Yorkshire pudding and peas. Mirvish is famous for his turkey giveaway every year on Thanksgiving.

## Loblaw Companies Ltd.

Theodore Primale Loblaw established the first store carrying his name in 1919 in Toronto. It pioneered the "self serve" concept, allowing customers to collect their own purchases, rather than asking for them at the counter. It is now one of the largest supermarket chains in the country, also owning Real Canadian Superstore, Extra Foods, Dominion, Atlantic Superstore, Fortinos, Maxi, No Frills, Provigo, Valu-Mart, Zehrs and Your Independent Grocer.

## Simpson's

Once one of Canada's best-known brands, Scotsman Robert Simpson started Simpson's in Toronto in 1872. Today Simpson's massive art deco Toronto location is the flagship Hudson's Bay store. It contains Arcadian Court, one of Canada's most opulent and expensive restaurants, first opened in Simpson's in 1929 (and partially restricted to men only for some time!). The Bay bought out Simpson's in 1978 and converted the last Simpson's stores to The Bay in 1991.

## Tim Hortons

The first Tim Hortons doughnuts were sold in 1964 from the chain's first store on Ottawa Street in Hamilton (it was originally just called "Tim Horton"). Its namesake, famed NHL player Tim Horton of Cochrane, Ontario, and a local police officer, Ron Joyce, were the original partners. After Horton's death in a car accident (in a police chase), Joyce took over. Today Tim Hortons is majority-owned by American fast-food giant Wendy's and has more than 2500 stores in Canada and 200 in the U.S. It is expanding into the U.K. and Ireland and recently became the biggest fast-food restaurant in Canada, passing McDonalds in sales and number of stores. An IPO of 29 million Tim Hortons share—15 percent of the company—was offered in March 2006.

A rival doughnut shop named for another famous hockey player—Eddie Shack Donuts—has only two stores, one each in Caledon and Guelph.

Below are some of Ontario's other coffee successes.

☞ Second Cup Coffee Ltd.—today Canada's largest coffee shop chain of the non-doughnut variety—started as a specialty coffee beans stand in Toronto's Yorkdale Mall in 1975.
☞ Coffee Time Donuts Inc., synonymous with Toronto's seedier neighbourhoods, originally started in Bolton and is now based in Scarborough. It operates more than 300 stores, including branches in Greece, Poland and China.
☞ Country Style Food Services is based in Richmond Hill.
☞ Timothy's World Coffee shops were started in London, Ontario, in 1975.

## CCM

The well-known maker of sports equipment, CCM—or Canadian Cycle and Motor Company Limited—was founded in Toronto in 1899.

### KRAFT

Fans of thin, highly processed cheese slices take note: James Lewis Kraft was born in Stevensville, Ontario, in 1874. In 1903, he moved to Chicago and started J.L. Kraft & Bros., which would go on to become the massive Kraft Foods company. In 1920, Kraft expanded back into Canada. Kraft introduced brands such as Miracle Whip, Jell-O, Maxwell House, Kool-Aid, Shake 'Ñ Bake and Cheez Whiz.

Kraft Dinner was released on an unsuspecting world in 1937 and took the public by storm. During the Second World War, it became popular when dairy foods were being rationed. In the U.S., it was renamed Kraft Macaroni and Cheese, and in the U.K., it was introduced as Kraft Cheesy Pasta. In Canada—the largest per capita consumer of Kraft Dinner in the world—it seems like the company didn't want to mess with a good thing, so it kept the original name.

The Barenaked Ladies' song "If I Had a Million Dollars" has a reference to Kraft Dinner in it. When the line comes up, fans regularly throw Kraft Dinner at the stage. The band started asking fans to donate the Kraft Dinner to food banks rather than throw it at them, especially after concert goers began throwing cooked mac and cheese.

## Purolator Courier Ltd.

Started in Toronto in 1960 as Trans Canadian Couriers Ltd., Purolator took on its current name in 1973. Now mostly owned by Canada Post, it is the biggest courier company in the country.

## Canada Life Assurance Company

The oldest insurance company in the country—Canada Life—started in Hamilton in 1846. Its Toronto headquarters is famous for a giant flashing light beacon. The set of lights on top of the sky scraper is actually a thermometer. When the lights on the beacon rise, the temperature is going up; when they fall, the temperature is predicted to drop. Green lights mean a clear sky, reds suggest cloudy, flashing red is rain and flashing white heralds snow.

## The Canada Company

Although the name isn't familiar, the Canada Company once owned much of southern Ontario. It was started in 1826 by John Galt (who also founded the city of Guelph) as a crown corporation to raise money for the government, which was still in debt for the War of 1812. The company bought up large tracts of land cheaply, then divided them and sold off plots. The Canada Company finally folded in 1951. Over the years, it had owned 1,384,000 hectares of land.

## STELCO

Tycoon Max Aiken, also known as Lord Beaverbrook, formed Stelco, originally called the Steel Company of Canada, in 1910. It merged five companies into the biggest steel maker in Canada and the defining feature of Hamilton.

## CANADA DRY

John J. McLaughlin launched the famous ginger-ale brand, Canada Dry, now owned by Cadbury-Schweppes, in Toronto in 1904. He started producing carbonated water in 1890, but it was "Canada Dry Pale Ginger Ale" that made his company a huge success (particularly taking off during the Depression, as a mixer to cover up the scent of booze). McLaughlin's father had founded MacLaughlin Motors, the precursor of Buick.

# Fast Food

Ontario has spawned a number of fast-food chains.

- ☞ Harvey's, the most successful Canadian burger restaurant, started in Richmond Hill in 1959.
- ☞ New York Fries, despite its name and checker cab–influenced décor, is actually based in Toronto.
- ☞ Pita Pit was opened in 1995 in Kingston.
- ☞ Mr. Sub opened in 1968 in Toronto.
- ☞ Yogen Früz, the frozen yogurt chain (whose name is not in any particular language), started in Toronto in 1986.

### Olympia & York Properties Corporation

The Toronto-based development company, owned by Austrian immigrant Paul Reichmann, is best known for going bankrupt over the Canary Wharf building project in London, U.K. It was the world's largest-ever property development and produced the three tallest buildings in the U.K. (the largest was called Canada Square).

# ROBBER BARONS AND DYNASTIES

*The old boy network is still too strong in Canadian business.*
*A visit to the Toronto clubs at lunch stands is about as great*
*a contrast to the multicultural, multiracial subway underneath*
*as can be humanly imagined. This is not healthy.*
—Bob Rae, former Ontario premier (1990–95), quoted 1996

## THE THOMSONS

Toronto resident Kenneth Thomson, who passed away in his
office on June 12, 2006, was the richest person in Canada
and the 15th richest in the world. He was responsible for
managing the Thompson family fortune, estimated to be
about $22 billion dollars. The media baron was also an actual
baron (specifically, the Second Baron of Fleet). He inherited
the Thomson Corporation from his father Roy Thomson
(for whom Roy Thomson Hall in Toronto is named). The
elder Thomson founded the family empire with a radio station in North Bay and with the purchase of the *Timmins
Press*. At various points, the company owned the *Globe and
Mail*, the *Times* (of London), the *Scotsman*, the *Jerusalem Post*
and CTV, as well as oil rigs in the North Sea, dozens of specialty publishing companies, medical and banking businesses,
and Toronto's Thomson Tower skyscraper. Kenneth Thompson
was well known as an art collector and was one of the main
benefactors to the Art Gallery of Ontario. A frugal man, he
admitted to saving store coupons and eating at McDonalds.

## THE WESTONS

Canada's second-richest person is Galen Weston, worth over
$8 billion. His grandfather founded a bakery empire in
Toronto. The Weston family now owns Loblaw Companies

Ltd., Holt Renfrew and Geroge Weston Bakeries Inc., as well
as the Selfridges and Co. department store chain in the UK.

## THE MASSEYS

Daniel Massey, a blacksmith in Newcastle, founded a company in 1847 that was to make his family one of the most
powerful in Canadian history. The Newcastle Foundry and
Machine Manufactory eventually became Massey-Harris Co.
and later Massey-Ferguson Ltd., the farm machinery giant.
It was one of Canada's first multinational corporations and
was at one point the largest farm machinery maker in the
Commonwealth, also producing bicycles and other machinery. The family was well known for philanthropy, funding
both Massey Hall and Massey College at the U of T.
Vincent Massey was Canada's first Canadian-born governor
general. Ever-unpopular businessman Conrad Black eventually bought the Massey-Ferguson company, and broke it up.
American giant AGCO Corp. now owns the remaining bits
of the company.

## THE AUSTINS

Irish immigrant James Austin (and others) founded the
Dominion Bank (which later became Toronto-Dominion)
and Consumers' Gas Company (which became Enbridge Gas
Distribution Inc.). The family lived in Spadina House, the
lavish mansion next to Casa Loma, which is now preserved
as a museum.

## JESSIE KETCHUM

The early 19th-century businessman made his fortune on
leather goods and real estate. He donated land to the city of
Toronto to develop Temperance Sreet, on the stipulation that
no alcohol be served there. "The Temperance Society," a slyly
named bar, operated during the early 21st century.

# FARMING

The best-known product of Ontario farming is the McIntosh apple. American immigrant John McIntosh discovered the apple when he cleared land in 1811 near Dundela, Ontario. The fruit of the tree was sweeter and juicier than most other apples, and McIntosh immediately began selling them. In 1835, he cloned the tree through grafting. By the 20th century, the McIntosh had become the most popular apple in North America, and today McIntoshes account for half of all apples grown in Canada. The original tree lived until 1910, and there is now a monument where it once stood. It's not known where the first tree came from—apple trees are not native to Ontario.

# Red Fife, or Not

Farmer and wheat breeder David Fife discovered one of Canada's best-known wheat strains near Peterborough in 1842. A friend of Fife's in Scotland sent him a seed packet that had come off a ship from Poland. Most of the wheat that Fife planted died, but the bit that remained produced better flour, had a higher yield and was more resistant to disease than any other known strain. Within a few years, Red Fife became the dominant wheat in Ontario, and later the Prairies. A new type, Marquis, bred partly from Red Fife, was until recently the most popular wheat in Canada. In 1905, the origins of Red Fife were discovered—it was actually an ancient Ukrainian variety called "Halychanka."

**MADE IN Ontario** It's appropriate that most of Canada's ketchup comes from the Heinz factory in Leamington— a town that bills itself as the "Tomato Capital of Canada" and has what it calls the Giant Tomato statue. The area around Leamington is known for its intensive hothouse tomato production. Every day, truckloads of tomatoes can be seen heading towards a squishy future at the ketchup factory.

"Ketchup" originally meant any sauce with vinegar and may come from the Chinese word *ke-tsiap*, meaning "eggplant sauce." It became popular in the west in the early 19th century.

**DID YOU KNOW?**

Although far behind Québec's output, Ontario is also known for its maple syrup. It takes 50 litres of maple sap to produce a single litre of syrup.

## Canadian National Exhibition

The Canadian National Exhibition, also called the CNE or the Ex, has been Toronto's annual fair since 1878. It was officially opened by Governor General the Marquis de Lorne, with the goal of promoting agriculture, gardening and industry. Crops of couch potatoes had their roots set at the Ex, too. Television was demonstrated for the first time at the 1938 Ex. A closed-circuit broadcast featuring an interview with boxers Jack Dempsey and Gordon Sinclair was transmitted from the Automotive Building to the Horticultural Building.

## Holland, not Holland

You'd be forgiven for thinking that the Holland Marsh area north of Toronto—set below sea level and drained by Dutch immigrants—was named after the Netherlands. In fact, the name of the small but remarkably rich farming area has nothing to do with that. Holland Marsh, the Holland River and the town of Holland Landing are all named after Major Samuel Holland, a British officer who surveyed the area in the late 18th century.

From the black earth of the Holland Marsh comes a range of garden goodness:

- ☛ 95 percent of Canada's celery crop,
- ☛ 80 percent of its carrots,
- ☛ 66 percent of its onions,
- ☛ 90 percent of all Asian vegetables sold in the Greater Toronto Area.

A study in 1999 showed that the Holland Marsh generates $265 million annually in vegetable sales, and directly employs 4770 people.

The dikes that prevent the marsh from flooding were originally built by burying old cars and anchoring them in place by planting willow trees on top of them.

DID YOU KNOW?

Peanuts can grow in Ontario. In the 1950s, they were introduced from the southern state of Georgia and first harvested in Ontario in 1955. They do well in the sandy soil of the tobacco belt, the area south of Tillsonburg.

## Quit Cigarettes... Try Ginseng Instead

You might not associate ginseng farming with Ontario, but a drive through the old tobacco belt in Norfolk County would prove otherwise. Jesuit priests discovered ginseng in Ontario in the 18th century. Today 220 ginseng farmers grow over 1,814,000 kilograms of ginseng in Ontario every year—more than anywhere else in North America. Most of it is exported to Asia, and as tobacco has become less popular, many tobacco farmers have switched to ginseng.

# NATURAL RESOURCES

The first oil well ever dug in North America was at Oil Springs, Ontario, in 1858, near the larger (also pretty aptly named) town of Petrolia and not far from Sarnia. The town is known for spurring the global oil industry, since many of its first technicians and business owners later travelled the world to open oil wells in Saudi Arabia, Texas, Alberta, Russia, Iran and elsewhere—a total of 87 countries in all. These men became known as "hard oilers." Oil is still being pumped at Petrolia, which now bills itself as "Canada's Victorian Oil Town."

**Gold in Them... Well, Right Under You, Actually**
The first gold rush in Canadian history started in 1866, near the town of Eldorado in eastern Ontario (funny how towns have such appropriate names). Gold was actually visible on the surface of some rock. One story says that a mine was discovered after a horse's hoof scraped away dirt to reveal gold. Another says that a fisherman left his spot by the river because the mosquitoes were getting too bad. His friend, who had been beside him, looked over and saw that the man had been sitting on a mound of gold. Few records were kept at the time—understandably, people were generally not interested in informing the government about their bonanzas. However, the gold didn't run deep, and before long, people moved on. In the 1980s, gold was discovered again nearby at Madoc, but so far attempts to open new mines have been commercial failures.

## Old Nick's Curse

That's what nickel was first called, because, though it looked kind of like silver, it was thought to be worthless.

But those early miners were wrong. Today, Sudbury's famous Big Nickel is there for a reason. Thirty percent of the world's nickel comes from the huge mines in that city, mostly left there as a result of an ancient meteorite.

Meteorite or not, just don't say the word "moonscape" around Sudburians. Residents are sensitive about the popular image of the city as a barren, cratered area left lifeless from mining pollution. At the time of Apollo, NASA conducted training exercises in Sudbury, but because of its rare shatter cone rock formations, not because it looked like the moon. Although the city has tried to get away from its "moonscape" image, nickel mining is still its biggest industry.

# Salt of the Earth

In 1865, while drilling for oil near Goderich, on the shore of Lake Huron, prospectors hit Canada's largest deposit of rock salt. Tunnels were soon set up, stretching deep underneath the lake, and today over half of Canada's salt comes from Lake Huron's salt mines. The importance of salt to the local economy is commemorated in Goderich's giant salt pillar monument (encased in glass, to keep it safe from rain, passing deer and whatnot). A nearby village is called Saltford.

**DID YOU**  **KNOW?**

Since 1975, amethyst has been the official mineral of Ontario. The world's largest mine of the beautiful, semi-precious purple stone is located near Thunder Bay.

# TAKE YOUR MEDICINE

## It Tastes Awful...And It Works!

That's the famous slogan of Buckley's Mixture, one of the last survivors of the age of patent medicines. W.K. Buckley, a Toronto pharmacist, invented it in 1920. The famous series of ads that emphasized its unpleasant taste began in 1986.

**Ontario** Dr. Frederick Banting, from Alliston, and his assistant, medical student Charles Best, are responsible for the most famous medical discovery in Canadian history. Together, at the University of Toronto in 1921, they invented insulin as a drug to treat diabetes. Banting won the Nobel Prize in 1923, along with J.J.R. Macleod, the head of the U of T's Physiology department. Upset that Best was left out, Banting publicly shared his prize with the student. Best later went on to become a professor and headed the Physiology department himself. The Banting and Best medical buildings at the U of T, side by side, are named after the two men.

### Norman Bethune

Possibly Ontario's most famous doctor ever—though he was virtually unknown during his lifetime—was Norman Bethune, who was born in Gravenhurst. Bethune studied medicine in Toronto and later taught at McGill University. His work in military hospitals during the Spanish Civil War and in China during the Japanese invasion made him famous. In Spain, he is credited with creating the modern military medical unit system, as well as inventing several new surgical tools, which were named after him. He was also an early supporter of public medicare. Bethune died in China in 1939 from an infection received from a patient he operated on. After his death, Chinese Communist leader Mao Zedong wrote an essay about Bethune's work, making the Canadian internationally known. A hospital in China is named after Bethune, as well as a school in Toronto and a college of York University. In Montréal, a statue of Norman Bethune stands near Concordia University. It is regularly decorated with flowers, and a conical, Chinese rice hat is sometimes placed on the statue's head.

DID YOU  KNOW?

The inventor of chiropractic health care was Daniel D. Palmer of Port Perry, Ontario. While he was an alternative medicine enthusiast living in Iowa, he developed the notion that various ailments were related to spinal problems. He went on to found the first chiropractic school.

## Dionne Quintuplets

On May 28, 1934, Yvonne, Annette, Cecile, Emilie and Marie Dionne were born near Corbeil, Ontario—the first quintuplets ever known to survive birth. Collectively, they weighed less than 6.5 kilograms. Despite the miracle of their birth, the five sisters were fated to have a tragic childhood. The government of Ontario infamously took the girls away from their impoverished family, and put them in a zoo-like structure in North Bay called "Quintland." There, under the management of Dr. Allan Roy Dafoe, who had supervised their birth, the quints were viewed through two-way mirrors by as many as 6000 people every day. Quintland—which briefly surpassed Niagara Falls as the largest tourist attraction in Canada—was credited with saving North Bay's economy during the Depression. Some suggested that Toronto's Casa Loma be refitted to house the girls and turn them into an even more fantastic tourist attraction. The quintuplets also appeared in commercials and several movies before being returned to their father, who they claimed sexually abused them. The quints later spoke out against their treatment and demanded compensation from the province. In 1998 the three surviving quintuplets, all living in Montreal, received a $4-million settlement from the Ontario government.

DID YOU KNOW?

Emily Stowe, born in Norwich, Ontario, was the first female doctor in Canada. Initially a teacher and married to Dr. John Stowe, she decided to become a doctor herself after her husband caught tuberculosis. In 1867, she graduated from the New York Medical College for Women (since no Canadian medical schools would accept women) and was licensed to practise in Ontario in 1880. Jenny Kidd Trout, a Scottish immigrant living in Stratford, graduated from Women's Medical College of Pennsylvania in 1875 and was licensed in Ontario in the same year. Stowe's daughter, Augusta Stowe, became the first woman to graduate from medical school in Canada in 1883.

# LAST CALL

## A Long Dry Spell

Prohibition lasted from 1916 to 1927 in Ontario. (By contrast, Prohibition lasted longest in PEI, from 1901 to 1948, and shortest in Québec, just for the year of 1919.) Even when the measure was ultimately repealed, the prohibition lobby was still strong enough in the infamously puritanical province that many forms of anti-alcohol legislation remained on the books. Here are some of Prohibition's echoes:

☛ Women were not allowed into bars without a man until 1970. Even when arriving with a male companion, women were forced to enter through a separate door and remain in a separate mixed-gender room, away from the main bar.

☛ Many towns and neighbourhoods remained dry long after Prohibition. Owen Sound—a port that once had an reputation for drunken rowdiness and was home to "Damnation Corners," a set of four particularly savage establishments—remained dry until 1961 (though the liquor business thrived in nearby Wiarton). Some Toronto neighbourhoods remained dry until the late 1990s.

☛ Oddly, it was illegal to stand up in a bar with a drink in your hand until 1970. Imagine getting arrested for a toast!

☛ Until the 1980s, limits on glass sizes and the number of drinks allowed on a table were still on the books.

☛ Bars could not be open on a Sunday until the 1980s.

☛ Last call for drinks was at midnight until 1998. It now sits at 2:00 AM.

☛ Toronto did not get its first outdoor patio where drinks were served until 1969, and the trend did not catch on until the 1980s.

☛ Illegal *coq au vin*, anyone? Restaurants were not allowed to cook with alcohol until the 1970s.

☛ "Bring your own booze" only became legal in Ontario in 2005 (though only for wine and not including homemade wine). It has yet to catch on.

### How 'Bout Another Prescription for the Road, Doc?

Enterprising Ontario residents often found ways around Prohibition. One way was to be prescribed "medicinal" alcohol by a friendly doctor. Between 1923 and 1924, some 810,000 prescriptions were written for "medicinal" alcohol. Alcohol could also be ordered by mail from provinces such as Québec and Sakatchewan, where it remained semi-legal. Finally, "standard hotels"—a euphemism for bars—began popping up. They were regulated by law and patrons were prohibited from ordering beer above 2.5 percent alcohol (which had to be ordered with food). Many, however, did not follow the rules. Because of the government monopoly, bootlegging still survives as a major industry in Ontario—

estimated at being worth $443 million annually and accounting for six percent of all liquor sales.

## A Drinking Problem?

Prohibition's most infamous relics are the Liquor Control Board of Ontario (or LCBO) and the Beer Store—the instruments of the provincial government's Big Brotherly concern for its citizens. The LCBO is the largest single buyer of booze in the world.

There were quirks in the system:

☛ The smaller and older Beer Stores in Ontario maintain the vaguely Stalinistic format of keeping the beer out of reach. Visitors to Ontario are often amazed to see customers looking over lists of brands on the wall, informing the clerk what they want and receiving their purchase out of the back room via a slot or conveyer belt.

☛ Earlier, the system was carried further. Customers had to write their alcohol choice on a card, along with their name and address, which was kept on file by the government.

# INVENTOR'S CORNER

## Birthplace of the Telephone?

One of the most famous inventions to be associated with Ontario is the telephone, but there is disagreement on how much of it was invented in the province. Alexander Graham Bell immigrated to Brantford, Ontario from Scotland and did much of his research on the invention there. However, he didn't unveil or patent the finished invention until he later moved to Boston. Bell made the first long-distance telephone call on August 10, 1876, from Brantford to Paris, Ontario, over 94 kilometres of cable.

The Guelph Elastic Hosiery Company invented the jock strap in the 1920s in Guelph. A contest was held to name the new invention. The winner received $5.

## Gideon Sundback, Fly Guy

Just think, how different the world would be without this invention—Swedish immigrant Gideon Sundback created the modern zipper in 1913 in St. Catharines. He patented it in 1917 as the "separable fastener." (Some predecessors to the zipper, using hooks and eye s rather than teeth, were in use earlier in the United States.)

## The Real McCoy?

Elijah McCoy, one of Ontario's most famous early black residents, was born in Essex County in 1884 to escaped slave parents. The family moved to Detroit when he was a child. McCoy was a lifelong inventor, best known for his steam-engine lubrication system. Some say McCoy's customers coined the slogan "the Real McCoy" in reference to this invention, but a lot of debate remains around the history of the phrase. McCoy also invented the lawn sprinkler and the folding ironing board.

Jazz organists, storefront churches and wedding chapels give praise! Morse Robb of Belleville invented the electric organ in the 1920s. The device replicated the sound of older church organs but without their huge size and pipes—making it cheaper and capable of running in any space. Robb was less successful in profiting from his organ—his company sold only 13 organs over five years, before shutting down.

### Roll Your Own

Painting your walls became a lot easier thanks to Norman Breakey, who patented the paint roller in 1940 in Toronto.

# It's About Time

Ever wonder where standard time—the system of time zones and a universally recognized official time—came from? Sir Sandford Fleming, a Scottish-born railway surveyor living in Ontario, first proposed the idea to the Royal Canadian Institute in 1879, but it was not formally adopted around the world until 1929. Before that, every town was responsible for setting its own time, using the sun.

### Light Bulb

Ever regret a decision you made? Imagine how University of Toronto medical student Henry Woodward must have felt. He and partner Matthew Evans invented a prototype of the light bulb in 1874, becoming the first person to produce light with electricity. Unable to find investors for his project, he sold the design to Thomas Edison, who improved it and patented it five years later, going on to make millions from it.

### BlackBerry

Research in Motion of Waterloo created the BlackBerry, an increasingly popular portable device used for phoning, e-mail and Internet access. Some say it's highly addictive—and have nicknamed it the "Crackberry."

# MUSIC

## Mr. New Year's

Big band leader Gaetano Alberto Lombardo—better known as Guy Lombardo—from London, Ontario, became one of the province's most famous musicians. Guy Lombardo and His Royal Canadians sold over 300 million albums and are most remembered for popularizing "Auld Lang Syne" as a New Year's song. A museum in London is now dedicated to Guy Lombardo.

## The Maple Leaf Forever

Alexander Muir of Toronto wrote Canada's alternative national anthem, "The Maple Leaf Forever," in 1867. He was inspired to write it when he saw leaves falling from the maple tree in his yard on Memory Lane, in the city's east end. The song became an instant hit in much of Ontario, but the over-the-top, pro-British theme of the lyrics made it unpopular with francophones. As a result, it lost out to Calixa Lavallée's "O Canada," which became the official national anthem in 1980.

In 1997, CBC Radio held a contest to select new lyrics for "The Maple Leaf Forever."

## GLENN GOULD

Canada's most famous pianist was born in Toronto in 1932.
He was best known for his brilliant performances of Bach
and for his personal eccentricities. These included refusing
to play unless he sat on a folding chair made by his father,
wearing heavy clothes much of the time and refusing to be
touched, as well as a fanatical obsession with scrambled eggs.
A lifelike statue of Gould sits on a bench in front of the
Glenn Gould Studio at the CBC headquarters in Toronto.

## AVRIL LAVIGNE

The pop star was born in Napanee in 1984. When Lavigne
wore a "Napanee Home Hardware" T-shirt on television, the
store was immediately deluged with calls from fans wanting
to buy one.

### Stan Rogers

The most famous Canadian Maritime folk singer was actually born in Hamilton, albeit to Nova Scotian parents. Although many of Rogers' songs were about the sea, he reportedly had no experience sailing and would easily get seasick.

### Barenaked Ladies

In their early days, the Ladies often tried to promote themselves by playing at CityTV's Speakers' Corner. The Toronto group first gained popularity after being removed from a list of bands playing at Toronto City Hall, because officials thought their name was offensive. When the city later tried to make it up to the band by offering them a key to the city, they refused. Their early hit "Be My Yoko Ono" won the band lawsuit threats from Yoko Ono herself—but a settlement was reached.

### Alanis Morissette

Alanis Morissette, most famous for her *Jagged Little Pill* album, grew up in Ottawa, where she showed an interest in singing early on. Her father, a school principal, had her sing the national anthem over the PA system every day. She also got a taste of stardom by performing as a child on the YTV kids' show, *You Can't Do That On Television*.

### Tragically Hip

Famous for their references to Canada and small-town life, the Tragically Hip started in Kingston in 1983. They were first signed to a record label after playing at Toronto's Horseshoe Tavern in 1987. Although the Hip are massively popular in Canada, they remain almost unknown elsewhere.

### Ronnie Hawkins

Called the founder of rock music in Canada, the hairy, shade-wearing Ronnie Hawkins was actually born in Arkansas. Connected to the early rock scene in the southern U.S., he moved to Peterborough in 1958.

# ART SHOW

## Tom Thomson

Tom Thomson is often considered the most famous member of the Group of Seven, despite never officially being part of it!

## A Grave Mystery

Thomson died in a mysterious canoe accident in Canoe Lake in 1917, three years before the Group of Seven formed. Known today as the ultimate Canadian nature painter, he had only been painting professionally for three years. Considering his famous skills as a canoeist and the calm weather at the time of his death, many people believed he was murdered. Friends buried him near the lake. Two days later, Thomson's family asked that he be dug up and reburied near his hometown of Leith. However, some people believe his body was never actually moved. Thomson's girlfriend continued to tend the original grave. Judge William Little published a book claiming that he had dug up Thomson's grave by the lake in 1956 and seen the remains! Medical testing later showed that the famous artist's bones were actually those of an aboriginal person.

## GROUP OF SEVEN

The members of the Group of Seven remain Canada's best-known artists. Their impressionistic pictures of rugged northern Ontario landscapes made Canadian art—previously thought of as an oxymoron—known across Canada and around the world. Officially formed in 1920, the group was made up of Franklin Carmichael, Lawren Harris, A.Y. Jackson, Frank Johnston, Arthur Lismer, J.E.H. MacDonald and Frederick Varley. The artists had studied in Europe but were keen to promote an art movement in Canada. Based in Toronto, they originally worked from a studio on Severn Street that still exists. Later, A.J. Casson, LeMoine FitzGerald and Edwin Holgate joined the group, making 10 members—though they kept the original name. In 1931, the Group of Seven disbanded, but most members formed a new association in 1933 called the Canadian Group of Painters. Of all the members of the Group of Seven, Lawren Harris' work changed the most over time—he eventually painted only brightly coloured, highly abstract works. The last surviving member of the group was A.J. Casson—he died in 1992.

## LORING AND WYLE

Although not as well known as the Group of Seven, Canada's most famous sculptors probably remain Frances Loring and Florence Wyle. Both Americans by birth, the two immigrated to Canada and spent most of their lives working from a studio in Toronto. They created many of the country's most famous First World War memorials, as well as the Robert Borden statue on Parliament Hill and the monuments at each end of the Queen Elizabeth Way.

## ROBERT BATEMAN

Prints of Robert Bateman's paintings are omnipresent in homes and offices everywhere. Probably Canada's best-known nature painter since the Group of Seven, Robert Bateman is known for his ultra-realistic depictions of wildlife. Bateman was born in Toronto. The high school that he once taught at in Burlington is now named after him.

## PAUL KANE

One of Canada's most famous 19th-century artists, Paul Kane was born in Toronto in 1810. He became famous for his scenes of the North and West. In 2002, one of Kane's paintings sold for $5 million to media tycoon Kenneth Thomson, the highest price ever paid for a Canadian artist's work.

# WRITING

## POET OF DEATH

John McCrae of Guelph is famous for writing "In Flanders Fields"—shortly before he ended up buried under poppies himself, during the First World War. He was never a professional poet and wrote only 29 poems—19 of them about death. "In Flanders Fields" immediately became one of the best-known poems of the war and was responsible for making the poppy an official symbol of remembrance in many countries.

## SUSANNA MOODIE AND CATHARINE PARR TRAILL

The two sisters, born in Britain, became Canada's best-known early authors, writing popular memoirs about life as settlers in Upper Canada. Both shared a certain outrage and disgust with their unrefined Canadian neighbours.

## STEPHEN LEACOCK

British immigrant Stephen Leacock became Canada's most famous humourist with the publication of *Sunshine Sketches of a Little Town* in 1912. Set in the fictional town of Mariposa, it was actually a satire on life in Orillia, and many of its anecdotes were inspired by stories from a local barber. The Stephen Leacock Award is still given to the best humour writers in Canada.

## FARLEY MOWAT

One of Canada's most resolutely Canadian writers, Port Hope resident Farley Mowat is loved (and hated) by many. He is known for his many books, mainly about the North, which often appeal to young people in particular. His works include *People of the Deer, Lost in the Barrens, Curse of the Viking Grave*, and *Never Cry Wolf*, which was made into a Disney movie. Newfoundlanders loathe him for *A Whale for the Killing*, because they were depicted as cruel killers of marine life. Inuit disliked *The Farfarers* because Mowat suggested early Europeans were first to build a civilization in the Canadian Arctic. Mowat is also famous for shooting at American warplanes with a shotgun from his backyard and for funding an alternative community newspaper in Port Hope after the existing one was bought by Conrad Black.

## MARGARET ATWOOD

Often thought of as Canada's most popular author, Margaret Atwood was born in Ottawa in 1939. She now lives in Toronto. Atwood is best known for *The Edible Woman*, *The Handmaid's Tale*, *Alias Grace* and *The Blind Assassin*. She also writes poetry and children's books and is a major landowner on Pelee Island, the southernmost inhabited place in Canada.

## SUPERMAN

Toronto-born Joe Shuster (cousin of the famous comedian Frank Shuster) invented Superman, the most popular comic book character of all time, while living in Cleveland, Ohio. Shuster had worked as a paperboy for the *Toronto Star* and named Superman's alter ego, Clark Kent, after his old boss at the paper.

## ARCHIBALD LAMPMAN

Probably the most famous anglophone poet of 19th-century Canada, Lampman was born in Morpeth in 1861. He's best known for his poems about nature and early life in Canada.

## MAZO DE LA ROCHE

Not well known today, but intensely popular in her time, Newmarket's Mazo de la Roche wrote the *Jalna* inspired by life at the Benares mansion in Mississauga.

# STAGE AND SCREEN

## Theatre Festivals

Many small towns and cities have tried to revive their economies with summer theatre festivals. Stratford, Ontario—home of the Stratford Festival—has probably been the most successful at it. Originally a rough industrial city and known as a railway junction and furniture manufacturing centre (and during the 1930s as the "Communist Capital of Canada" because of its militant labour movement), Stratford went into decline after World War II. The city rebranded itself as a tourist destination and a centre for the arts with the 1953 launch of the Stratford Festival. In 1962, the Shaw Festival had similar success in Niagara-on-the-Lake.

### JAY SILVERHEELS

Jay Silverheels, born Harold Smith, played Tonto on *The Lone Ranger* and appeared in a number of other westerns. He has a star on the Hollywood Walk of Fame. Silverheels was born in 1919 on the Six Nations Reserve.

### TRUSTY SCOUT?

Tonto frequently called the Lone Ranger *kemo sabe*—and the meaning of the word, first used by original radio show director Jim Jewell, has been hotly debated. It almost certainly means nothing, but here are a few possible explanations.

☞ The official story from the show's creators is that it means "trusty friend" and was copied from the name of a boys' summer camp, Kamp Kee-Mo-Sah-Bee.

☞ In the Tewa language, *kemo sabe* supposedly means "Apache friend."

☞ In Apache, the phrase means "white shirt."

☞ In Yavapai, *kinmasaba* means "one who is white."

- In the Minnesota Ojibwa dialect, *giimoozaabi* means "he who peeks" or could also mean "scout."
- In Navajo, *kemosabe* supposedly means "soggy bush."
- In Spanish, *qui no sabe* means "he who knows nothing." *Tonto* also means "stupid" in Spanish slang.
- In Japanese martial arts terminology, *ki musubi* means to unite one's energy with that of one's opponent.

## AMERICA'S SWEETHEART
Born in Toronto in 1892 as Gladys Louise Smith, Mary Pickford became one of the greatest Hollywood silent movie stars, nicknamed "America's Sweetheart." She was married for a time to famous director Douglas Fairbanks. Before her death in 1979, Pickford successfully petitioned the Canadian government to restore her citizenship.

## DAN AYKROYD
Comedian and actor Dan Aykroyd was born in Ottawa and studied criminology at Carleton University. His father, Samuel Aykroyd, was a policy advisor to Pierre Trudeau.

## SARAH POLLEY
One of Canada's best-known actresses, Sarah Polley was born in Toronto. She is best known for her role on the television series *Road to Avonlea* (which was set in Prince Edward Island but actually filmed in Uxbridge, Ontario).

## KAREN KAIN
Canada's most famous ballerina was born in Hamilton in 1951, the same year that the National Ballet of Canada was established in Toronto.

## MIKE MYERS
The star of the *Austin Powers* movies and longtime *Saturday Night Live* member, Mike Myers grew up in Scarborough. A street, Mike Myers Drive, is named after him.

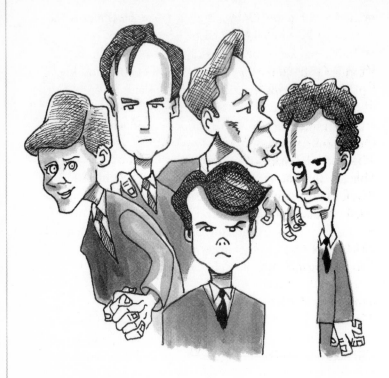

## KIDS IN THE HALL

One of Canada's most popular comedy series of all time, *The Kids in the Hall*, was filmed in Toronto and contained a number of local references. Three of the five members of the group—Dave Foley, Scott Thompson and Mark McKinney— were from Ontario.

## JIM CARREY

Well-known rubber-faced comedian Jim Carrey was born in Newmarket and grew up in Scarborough.

## TOM GREEN

Gross-out comic Tom Green was born in Pembroke and got his start with a local cable show in Ottawa.

# IN THE NEWS

## PETER GZOWSKI

Peter Gzowski—nicknamed "Mr. Canada"—was born in Toronto and went on to become *Maclean's* magazine's youngest editor and the host of CBC Radio's *Morningside*. He was the great-grandson of Polish immigrant Sir Casimir Gzowski. The elder Gzowski, a world-renowned engineer, was responsible for building the first railway bridge over the Niagara River, as well as many other projects in Ontario. He was briefly Ontario's lieutenant-governor.

## MACLEAN'S

Toronto businessman John Bayne Maclean founded the magazine that became *Maclean's* in 1905. It was originally named *The Business Magazine* and later, *The Busy Man's Magazine*.

## PETER JENNINGS

A household name in the United States, Peter Jennings was the nightly news anchor on ABC from 1978 to 2005. He was born in Toronto, the son of Charles Jennings, the first CBC Television anchor. He died of lung cancer in 2005.

## MARY ANN SHADD CARY

Mary Ann Shadd Cary is famous for being the world's first female newspaper editor. A black immigrant from the United States, she started *The Provincial Freeman* in 1853, a newspaper aimed at Canadian blacks and promoting immigration to Canada through the Underground Railroad.

# IN THE CLOUDS

## Size Does Matter...to Tourists

The Canadian National Railway built Ontario's most famous
building—the CN Tower—in 1973 as a 533.33-metre-high
television broadcast tower. But it became obsolete almost
immediately, because cable overtook broadcast as the most
popular form of television. As a result, few buildings near the
height of the CN Tower have been built in the past 30 years.
That is set to change soon, though, as Dubai, in the United

Arab Emirates, builds the Burj Dubai skyscraper, a 705-metre office tower set to open in 2008.

Since the early 1970s, the CN Tower's main purpose has been to fulfill the role of Toronto's biggest tourist attraction (no pun intended). In 1995, when CN Railway was privatized, there was public opposition to the tower falling into private (or worse, American) hands. So the CN Tower was broken off from CN and is now owned by Canada Lands Company, a crown corporation used for federal government real estate holdings. "CN" now officially stands for "Canada's National" as opposed to "Canadian National." Television and radio signals are still broadcast and it is also used as a cellphone tower.

The CN Tower is—for the moment—the tallest freestanding building on land in the world. It's sometimes incorrectly touted as being the tallest building of any type. In fact, there are many radio and television towers taller than the CN Tower. All of them are supported with guy wires, though, and so can't be considered freestanding. For the record, the tallest structure ever built was the Warsaw Radio Mast in Poland at 646.38 metres, though it collapsed in 1991. Today, the tallest structure is the KVLY-TV mast in North Dakota. The Petronius Platform, an oil rig in the Gulf of Mexico, is 610 metres tall and is considered the tallest freestanding structure in the world, though most of it is underwater.

The CN Tower has 1776 steps. Annual races up the stairs are held to raise money for charity. The record time for fastest climb from the ground to the first viewing deck is seven minutes, 52 seconds. The tower's revolving restaurant isn't nearly as fast—it takes 72 minutes to make one rotation.

In 1999, New Yorker Ashrita Furman became the first person to climb the CN Tower's stairs on a pogo stick, completing the ascent in 57 minutes, 51 seconds. (Furman holds

32 Guinness world records, in categories such as hula hoop racing, milk bottle balancing and underwater juggling.)

In 1979, Norman Alexander and Joe Squire carried a 200-kilogram piano up the CN Tower stairs. It took them seven and a half hours.

In 1984, stuntman Roger Brown, rolled down the entire staircase while covered in padding. Ouch. It took him one hour, 51 minutes. In the same year, another stuntman, Terry McGauran, drove a motorcycle up the stairs in less than an hour.

The CN Tower was the site of the world's longest yodel, performed by Donn Reynolds in 1980. He belted out the seven-hour and 29-minute performance over the city from the roof of the Skypod level.

**Casa Loma**
Sir Henry Pellatt, a military officer and hydroelectric tycoon, built Toronto's largest and most eccentric existing home, Casa Loma. In 1911, he made plans to build the lavish $3.5-million medieval-style castle, overlooking Toronto from Spadina Hill. It featured a secret passage between Pellatt's office and his wine cellar, and an underground tunnel connecting the castle with its stables.

But the First World War and some bad business decisions nearly bankrupted Sir Henry. When property taxes increased, Pellatt was forced to sell the still incomplete Casa Loma and move to his more modest country home. The castle spent a brief period as a luxury hotel, but it failed with the onset of the Great Depression. Numerous other concepts were floated, including a high school, a war veterans' home, a convent, an Orange Order lodge and even a new home for the popular (and state-owned) Dionne quintuplets. Since 1937, Casa Loma has been a tourist attraction, re-creating

Sir Henry's decade of opulence. Before his death in 1939, the impoverished Pellatt visited Casa Loma himself as an ordinary guest and signed the guest register. He died with $185.08 in the bank and $6000 in debts.

The name "Casa Loma" means "house on the hill" in Spanish. The property's previous owner, who had planned to build a house there, coined the name.

# Official Residences

Ottawa is home to several impressive official residences.

☛ Rideau Hall, home of Canadian Governors General, was originally built as a middle-class stonemason's home in 1838. In 1864, the government began renting it as a home for the Queen's representative in Canada. Later it was bought and expanded. The grounds around Rideau Hall used to house a unique toboggan slide, and the building once housed an indoor tennis court. La Citadelle in Québec City is the other official residence of Governors General.

☛ Canadian prime ministers reside at 24 Sussex Drive. The original name for the house, built in 1866, was Gorffwysfa, meaning "place of rest" in Welsh, but the government did not use the name after buying it in 1943. It is left to each prime minister to furnish the house, sometimes resulting in scandalous overspending, not to mention fashion crimes. Pierre Trudeau installed a pool and Brian Mulroney installed leopard carpeting.

☛ Stornoway—at 541 Acacia Avenue—is the residence of leaders of the official opposition. It was built in 1914, and named after a house in Scotland. Lucien Bouchard, while leader of the Bloc Québecois, refused to live there, staying in Hull instead. Reform Party leader Preston Manning suggested that it be sold or turned into a bingo hall, but eventually chose to move in.

☛ The federal government bought 7 Rideau Gate in 1966 to use as a guesthouse for foreign heads of state and other distinguished visitors.

**Chorley Park**
Did the Ontario government ever have its equivalent of Rideau Hall? Toronto's most lavish home—built as a residence for Ontario's lieutenant-governors—was constructed in 1915 and designed in the style of French castles. During the Depression, the public resented such displays of opulence, so the province abandoned the building in 1937. In 1960, it was demolished. Today, lieutenant-governors have a residence inside Queen's Park. Premiers and leaders of the Opposition must buy or rent their own houses (albeit with considerable financial support from the public).

# Sharon Temple

The Temple of the Children of Peace, commonly known as the Sharon Temple, is one of Ontario's oddest buildings. It seems both plain and extraordinary at the same time. It was built by the Children of Peace, a break-off group of the Quakers, led by the charismatic David Willson, between 1825 and 1832. The group established a colony called Hope, centred around the temple and featuring other similar buildings. The temple is built in the traditional plain clapboard style of Quaker meeting houses but is set up like a ziggurat or pyramid with diminishing storeys. Willson believed it to be a re-creation of Solomon's Temple from the Old Testament. It was square (to show square dealing,) its three storey represented the Trinity, and its 12 pillars represented the 12 apostles.

**DID YOU KNOW?**

The Children of Peace shared their property and were known for starting the first homeless shelter in Ontario. They also started the first non-military band in Canada, which sat in the upper storeys of the temple to play. During the 1837 uprising, members of the sect were known for becoming the most militant of the rebels. In fact, Samuel Lount, one of two men hanged for his role, was a member of the Children. They also fervently supported William Lyon Mackenzie. When Mackenzie was elected in their riding, they marched with him all the way to Toronto on foot, several days' walk. When David Willson died in 1866, the sect quickly declined and disappeared.

It's hard to believe today, but when the Royal York Hotel was built in 1927, it towered over Toronto's skyline and was advertised as "the tallest building in the British Empire."

**DID YOU KNOW?**

The SkyDome (now rather awkwardly named the Rogers Centre) was completed in 1989 and was the first building in the world with a completely retractable roof. The roof is actually made up of four panels that move separately. As well as hosting concerts and other events, it's home to Major League Baseball's Blue Jays and the Canadian Football League's Argonauts (and was briefly home to the National Basketball Association's Raptors).

☛ It is the only major stadium in the world with a hotel built into it, including 70 rooms overlooking the field. There are many stories of the crowd's attention being drawn away from sports action to action of another type in the hotel room windows, sometimes with the help of the giant Jumbotron screen—the largest of its kind in North America.

☞ The biggest crowd ever at Rogers Centre was drawn by Wrestlemania X8 in 2002, when 68,237 wrestling fans showed up.

☞ It is the tallest Major League Baseball stadium at 31 storeys, although often the least attended.

☞ In 1992, it made a world record for the most hot air balloons in an enclosed space—46!

☞ It takes 16 hours to convert the field between baseball and football games.

☞ The original mascot for the stadium was ridiculously named "Domer the Turtle."

☞ The sculpture of jeering fans attached to the side of the Rogers Centre is called "The Audience" and was created by famous Toronto artist Michael Snow.

☞ The Rogers Centre's Hard Rock Café is home to North America's largest electric guitar.

☞ Since opening, 800 kilometres of hot dogs have been sold in the Rogers Centre.

☞ Since the Blue Jays' World Series victories in 1992 and 1993 and the Major League Baseball strike, attendance has declined at the stadium. In an attempt to entertain fans, the Rogers Centre's management experimented with something called the "Hot Dog Blaster" in 2000. A bazooka-like device, it fired hot dogs into the stands, pulverizing them in the process and raining down pork chunks on the crowd.

☞ The Rogers Centre replaced the (open-roofed) Exhibition Stadium, a short-lived structure known as "the mistake by the lake." In 1979, the Blue Jays played the first Major League Baseball game to take place on a completely snow-covered field.

# Palladium

Opened in 1996, the National Hockey League's Ottawa Senators arena was originally named the Palladium. It later became the Corel Centre and finally the Scotiabank Place. The giant letters that once made up the Palladium sign were auctioned off (one Ottawa resident, in a fit of self-promotion, bought her initials to display in her front yard.)

 Maple Leaf Gardens in Toronto is now set to become a supermarket, after Loblaw bought it. The famous NHL arena sold out every hockey game from 1949 to 1999, before the Leafs moved to the Air Canada Centre. The Gardens once featured a gondola that sportscasters sat in, which was eventually destroyed by infamous team owner Harold Ballard. Ballard also tore down the Queen's portrait, saying: "She doesn't buy tickets, does she?" He made the team the most profitable in the NHL but gained an awful reputation for trading its best players, insuring its failure to be successful on the ice. He was also remembered for calling CBC TV personality Barbara Frum "a dumb broad."

## OCAD Building
Possibly the province's most absurd and gravity-defying structure, Toronto's Sharp Centre for Design appears to be suspended above the Ontario College of Art and Design (OCAD). This "floating shoebox" is held up by a number of brightly coloured pillars.

# Bata Shoe Museum

A building that is actually meant to look like a shoebox, and in a manner of speaking is a sort of shoebox, is the Bata Shoe Museum in Toronto. The museum was established by the Bata family, Czech immigrants and founders of the huge

Bata Shoe Company. It was established in 1995 and is one of the only museums dedicated to historic footware.

The Bata Shoe Museum was the scene of a massive theft on January 22, 2006. Thieves made off with a pair of jewelled 18th-century Indian slippers worth $160,000, a gold toe ring worth $11,000 and a gold anklet worth $45,000. A month later, the loot was recovered and the thief caught after he tried to develop pictures of the stolen footware in a photo shop only blocks away from the museum.

**DID YOU**  **KNOW?**

The gothic revival CHUM Building is famous for being home to MuchMusic (and Speakers' Corner) and CityTV. It was previously a Methodist office building and a Bible printing factory.

# SPORTS MANIA

*"Catch Me"*

—Slogan for disgraced Olympic sprinter Ben Johnson's line of clothing,
launched 2005.

## The Great One

An Ontario athlete who needs positively no introduction,
Wayne Gretzky was born in Brantford in 1961. The following
are among his more remarkable achievements and doings.

☛ At age 10, he played in a local hockey league, scoring 378
goals in 85 games.

- Gretzky started wearing his trademark number 99 jersey while playing for the Sault Ste. Marie Saints (he apparently wanted number nine—Gordie Howe's number—but had to settle for 99, because nine was already taken).

- In 1979, Edmonton Oilers owner Peter Pocklington signed Gretzky to a 21-year personal services contract, the longest in hockey history. The personal services contract—as opposed to a traditional player's contract—allowed the Oilers to keep Gretzky when they moved from the Western Hockey League to the NHL. However, the contact was mutually terminated in 1988, allowing Gretzky to be sold to the Los Angeles Kings.

- During his NHL career, Gretzky set season records for the most goals scored, the most assists and the most points.

- He was the first player to average more than two points per game over the course of a season and the only player to reach 200 points in a season (he did this five times). He also holds the record for most career points.

- In the 1983–84 season, Gretzky scored in 51 consecutive games—another NHL record. Three times in his career, he scored 50 goals in 50 games.

- A part owner of the Blue Jays and a fan of the team, Gretzky lobbied Toronto City Hall to rename part of Peter Street (which leads to the Rogers Centre) Blue Jays Way. He also convinced the city to realign the street numbers so that his sports bar on the street, Wayne Gretzky's, would become 99 Blue Jays Way.

- Gretzky has been immortalized in the form of a distinctly unhealthy drink—a "Gretzky" is a coffee with nine sugars and nine creams in it.

ONLY IN ONTARIO

Conn Smythe—owner, general manager and coach all in one—bought the Toronto St. Patricks on Valentine's day in 1927 for $200,000, and renamed them the Toronto Maple Leafs. They were to become the most profitable team in hockey history, winning their first Stanley Cup in 1932.

# "He Shoots, He Scores!"

Toronto sports journalist Foster Hewitt coined hockey's best-known catchphrase: "He shoots, he scores!" In 1923, Hewitt was the second person to do commentary on a hockey game (after Saskatchewan's Pete Parker). Famous for perching on a gondola over the ice at Maple Leaf Gardens, Hewitt finished his career by covering the famous 1972 Canada–Soviet Union series.

MADE IN Ontario The hockey net was invented in Beamsville in 1897. William Fairbrother, goalie for the Beamsville Senior Hockey Team, draped a fishing net around the back of his goal posts. The net was so popular, that within a few years every rink was using one.

# Bobby Orr

Also among hockey's greatest players was Bobby Orr of Parry Sound. Orr holds records for most points and assists by a defenceman. He is widely considered the best defenceman of all time.

### The Stratford Streak

Ontario also produced one of the first great stars of hockey—Howie Morenz. Morenz, born in Mitchell and raised in Stratford, was known as the "Mitchell Meteor" and the "Stratford Streak." He started his professional career with the Montréal Canadiens in 1923, but his career ended tragically when he died from leg injury complications in 1937.

### The First Grey Cup

The Canadian Football League's first Grey Cup championship game—named after the cup donated by Governor General Earl Grey—was held in Toronto in 1909. The University of

Toronto Varsity Blues defeated Toronto Parkdale 26–6.
The Grey Cup was originally meant to be awarded to the
best rugby team in Canada, but the Canadian variant of
rugby, under American influence, later evolved into
Canadian football.

## Tom Longboat

The famous Onandaga long-distance runner Tom Longboat,
also known as Cogwage e, was born on the Six Nations
Reserve in 1887. His first major victory was in the Around
the Bay Race in Hamilton in 1906, and he went on to win
the Boston and New York marathons. In the First World
War, Longboat worked as a dispatch runner for the Canadian
army. Today, a street in Toronto is named after him, and
the Tom Longboat Award is given out annually to the best
aboriginal athlete in Canada. He continues to be known as
Canada's greatest marathoner.

DID YOU  KNOW?

When it's not being held aloft, the Grey Cup lives in the Canadian Football Hall of Fame in Hamilton.

## Row, Row, Row Your...Football?

The Toronto Argonauts is Toronto's oldest existing sports team. They were founded in 1873—as a branch of the (also still existing) Toronto Argonaut Rowing Club.

 Canada's first major racecar track was Mosport International Raceway, built in Bowmanville in the 1950s.

## Ben Johnson

The famous sprinter is best known for losing his gold medal after being accused of doping in the 1988 Seoul Olympics. Caught again later on, he was disqualified for life from racing. Left out of mainstream sport, Johnson made some odd career move, later working as a soccer coach for the son of Libyan dictator Muammar Qaddafi. In Italy in 2000, he was supposedly outrun by a group of Roma children who had stolen his wallet.

## Ned Hanlan

Canada's greatest rower, Hanlan grew up on the Toronto Islands. He is said to have lost only six of his 300 races, which took place on three continents. Today, a statue of him stands on Hanlan's Point, near Toronto Islands Airport.

DID YOU KNOW?

James Naismith of Almonte, Ontario, invented basketball. He came up with the game in 1892 while teaching in the United States. Peach bushel baskets were originally used as baskets, and initially the game had several different rules from today. Players could only pass the ball, for instance, rather than dribbling it. Naismith went on to coach basketball at the University of Kansas, where he became the only coach in the history of the university with a losing record! When basketball was officially added to the Olympics in 1936, Naismith handed out the medals. He is also remembered for designing the first helmet for American football.

**Babe Ruth**
Babe Ruth's first professional home run was hit in the old baseball park on Toronto Island, against the Toronto Maple Leafs baseball team.

# The Other Toronto Maple Leafs

That's the baseball team, not the hockey team. Founded in 1886 as the Toronto Canucks, and known from 1896 to 1968 as the Toronto Maple Leafs, the team was one of the major fixtures in the International League (the level immediately below Major League Baseball). From 1952–56, they led the league in attendance, but moved to Louisville, Kentucky in 1968. In 1969, the modern-day Toronto Maple Leafs baseball team was founded as an amateur team in the Intercounty Baseball League to play in Christie Pits Park.

**Beachville Baseball?**
The first recorded game of baseball in Canada—and possibly the first game of modern baseball in the world—happened on June 4, 1838, in Beachville, south of London. This was a year

before the "official" invention of baseball in Cooperstown, New York, by Abner Doubleday. However, most modern historians believe that the game dates back much further than either event. Primordial stick and ball games in North America and Europe go back at least 100 years earlier. So when did baseball become baseball? That's one question that sports historians still can't answer.

## Five-Pin Bowling

A pint-sized variation on conventional bowling, five-pin bowling was invented in Toronto in 1909. The idea was to increase the sport's popularity and allow it to be played more quickly, on lunch breaks or after work. Five-pin bowling remains more popular in Canada than anywhere else.

**DID YOU**  **KNOW?**

In 1954, 16-year-old Marilyn Bell of Toronto became the first person to swim across Lake Ontario, polishing off the 52 kilometres in just under 21 hours. Bell later swam the English Channel and the Juan de Fuca Strait, between Vancouver Island and mainland British Columbia.

## Vicki Keith

Vicki Keith, considered to be one of the world's greatest long-distance swimmers, later upstaged Marilyn Bell. Keith made a double crossing of Lake Ontario in 1987. In 1988, she swam all the Great Lakes—a total of 290 kilometres. She appears several times in the *Guinness Book of World Records* for swimming the butterfly stroke for nearly 81 kilometres in Lake Ontario (at the age of 44), swimming for almost 130 hours straight in Kingston Pool and swimming 67.5 kilometres in 24 hours.

# Major Figures

☞ Elvis Stojko, two-time world champion figure skater, is from Richmond Hill.

☞ Brian Orser of Belleville won the 1987 world championship in figure skating.

☞ Barbara Ann Scott of Toronto was the first Canadian woman to win a figure-skating gold. She did it in 1948 in St. Moritz, Switzerland.

# George Chuvalo

Called "the toughest man I ever fought" by Muhammad Ali, Toronto's George Chuvalo was Canadian heavyweight boxing champion. He lost twice to Ali—but without being knocked out and after 15 and 12 rounds—no small feat, to say the least. Chuvalo was supposedly part of the inspiration for the title character of the *Rocky* movies.

## Pro Wrestlers

Whipper Billy Watson, also known as William Potts, of Toronto was the two-time world wrestling champion, in 1946 and 1956, and claimed to have won 99 percent of the 6400 matches he competed in during his 30-year career. Fans of the outrageous world of professional wrestling will also recognize the name Tiger Ali Singh or Tiger Jeet Singh—the stage monikers of Gurjit Singh Hans—the famous Indo-Canadian wrestler, also from Toronto.

# Lennox Lewis

Lennox Lewis (who was born in the U.K., but grew up in Kitchener) won the Olympic gold medal for boxing for Canada in 1988. After returning to the U.K., he became a world champion in professional boxing.

# HIGHER LEARNING

## ROCHDALE COLLEGE

One of the most remarkable and absurd things ever to have happened in Toronto, Rochdale College was an experiment in education and housing that ran between 1968 and 1975. It was Canada's first and only major free university. The 18-storey high-rise was built as a University of Toronto student residence, but a surplus in student housing led to it being turned over to a group of alternative-minded professors, students and hippies. The result was a combination dorm and university that offered no set schedules, no set enrollment and few set rules. Police hated the college for its role in the drug culture and because it used Hells Angels as security guards. It was said to be the number one source of marijuana, hashish and LSD in North America. Different floors are rumoured to have competed against each other to cultivate new strains of marijuana. Some other Rochdale achievements and infamies (before it was shut down after violence caused by bikers) included the following:

☛ In one of the most famous jibes at traditional universities, no degrees were normally conferred at Rochdale. However, you could get a bachelor's degree if you paid $25 and answered a skill-testing question. To get a master's degree, you had to pay $50 and you could choose the question. To get a PhD, the fee was $100 and no questions were asked.

☛ "Non-degrees" were also offered. For $100 and a promise to say nothing you could get a "non-PhD." For $50 and for saying something logical, you could get a "non-MA." For $25 and saying something useful, a "non-BA" was offered.

☛ Hundreds of homeless people took advantage of Rochdale's openness, sleeping in empty dorm rooms every night. When the decision was made to lock the doors and issue keys to students only, keys fetched as much as $25 on the street.

- Hippies met police raids with confetti, balloons and on one occasion, a cake reading "Welcome 52 Division."
- Rochdale residents launched some of Toronto's most enduring cultural institutions, including Coach House Press, House of Anansi Press, Theatre Passe Muraille and Toronto Free Dance Theatre.
- The college also launched CRUD, a radio station often at odds with the CRTC.
- Dennis Lee, famous children's book author and poet (later to win the Governor General's Award and become Poet Laureate of Toronto) got his start as a faculty member at Rochdale. Renowned organic farmer and writer Brewster Kneen also "taught" at Rochdale. Rosie Rowbotham, a Rochdale character and hanger-around (who would later become a CBC producer) was sentenced to 20 years in jail—the longest sentence ever in Canada—for selling marijuana.

☞ When Toronto film archivist Reg Hartt screened films at Rochdale, he offered free entry to anyone who came nude.

☞ The building is now Senator David A. Croll Apartments, a public housing tower block. A sculpture outside is called "The Unknown Student" and looks despondent, perhaps having just come out of an exam at some non-free university.

## University of Toronto

Founded in 1827 as King's College, the University of Toronto is the oldest university in Ontario and the largest in Canada.

☞ Originally an Anglican university, under the auspices of Upper Canada's Anglican oligarchy, it became secular in 1848. Disgruntled Anglicans broke away to form the University of Trinity College, but it was later reunited with the U of T. The old Trinity College campus was torn down and is now Trinity Bellwoods Park. Only its gates remain.

☞ The U of T's Robarts Library is the main part of what is the third largest university library system in North America. An odd, awkward-looking structure, built mostly out of concrete in a brutalist style, a popular student legend says that Robarts is sinking into the ground because its architects forgot to account for the weight of books in its design.

☞ University College—one of the main buildings at the U of T—was originally meant to face east, but was built facing south to save an old tree. The tree no longer stands.

☞ The U of T's bookstore and student centre was once Toronto's central library.

☞ The university has a bad reputation for large class sizes— some first-year classes contain over 1200 students and take place in the huge Convocation Hall.

# YORK UNIVERSITY

Buried in the vast suburban sprawl of Toronto, York is Canada's third-largest university by number of students. It has the largest campus of any university in Canada.

- ☞ "If you can use a fork, you can go to York" is an old rhyme jokingly used by students to describe the university's low-grade requirements. However, York has recently become much more renowned academically.
- ☞ In 2005, professor David Noble decided to protest York's policy of cancelling classes for Christian and Jewish holidays, which he felt was discriminatory to non-Christian or non-Jewish students. After attempting to teach through the holidays, he received a number of threats from students, causing him to briefly change his policy to cancelling classes on all religious holidays of any type—resulting in very few days of teaching.
- ☞ Located in an open, somewhat desolate setting, York's campus is infamous for its high winds, especially in the winter. An urban legend among students is that the original buildings were designed by a California architect who had spent much of his career trying to increase wind in hot climates.

## OTHER INSTITUTIONS OF HIGHER LEARNING

☛ Wilfrid Laurier University was previously known as Waterloo Luthern University. It changed its name when it became secular, supposedly choosing Wilfrid Laurier so it could maintain the name initials.

☛ Queen's University has a reputation for academic selectiveness and long-standing traditions—some of them odd. Students are issued tam-o'-shanter hats, in recognition of the school's Scottish heritage, and compete every year to climb a greased poll. The school further developed its blue-blooded reputation by opening a campus in England, in a castle donated by one of its alumni. That reputation was set back somewhat by the 2005 homecoming riots, in which rowdy students flipped over and burned a car and threw bottles at police.

☞ An asteroid—Uwontario—is named after the University of Western Ontario in London. Students at other universities have referred to the school as the "University of Wealthy Ontarians," on account of its posh reputation.

☞ The University of Ottawa—the third biggest in Ontario after the U of T and York—is also the largest and oldest bilingual university in North America. It is often confused with Ottawa University—which is located in Kansas.

☞ University of Waterloo math students have great and inexplicable devotion to a 15-metre-long pink tie—the unofficial symbol of their faculty. Earlier giant pink ties were stolen by a group calling itself the Tie Liberation Organization (TLO) and by the hated rivals of math students—engineers. The engineering faculty has its own symbol—a 20-metre-long wrench known as the "rigid tool" after the Rigid Tool Company, which donated it. Queen's engineering students stole it in 1982, but returned it encased in concrete. Waterloo holds the record for the longest trip made with a solar-powered car. In 2004, the Midnight Sun VII travelled 15,079 kilometres across North America over 40 days.

☞ The motto of Brock University is "*Surgite!*" or "Push on!" These were supposedly the last words of Major General Isaac Brock, military commander during the War of 1812. The less-than-inspiring phrase, "If you can walk and talk, you can go to Brock," has been applied to the university.

☞ The tiny University of Ontario Institute of Technology in Oshawa is the newest university in the province, started in 2003.

# TRIBUTE TO TREBEK

*Will you adopt me?*

—child contestant to Alex Trebek

## Alex Trebek

*The Bathroom Book of Ontario Trivia* would be sorely remiss if it didn't pay tribute to the greatest figure in the history of trivia, *Jeopardy!* host Alex Trebek. Bilingual Trebek was born Giorgi Suka-Alex Trebek in 1940 in Sudbury, to a Franco-Ontarian mother and a Ukrainian father. He has a degree in philosophy from the University of Ottawa and started out as a CBC newscaster. The CBC later gave him his first game show, *Reach for the Top*. After moving to the U.S and before taking over the reins at *Jeopardy!*, Trebek hosted a number of game shows, including the wonderfully named *Wizard of Odds*. The game-show wizard now lives in California and runs a farm there.

- ☛ Trebek has hosted over 4000 episodes of *Jeopardy!*
- ☛ He has a star on the Hollywood Walk of Fame and three Daytime Emmy awards.
- ☛ The game show host has been an advocate for the welfare of Alaskan muskox.
- ☛ He has a sense of humour. Trebek once appeared on an *X-Files* episode as himself, suggesting that he lived a double life as a government agent who intimidated UFO abductees to keep them from talking about their experiences.

# ABOUT THE AUTHOR

## René Josef Biberstein

René Biberstein was born in Toronto and spent part of his childhood in Switzerland. He studied journalism at Concordia University, won the Concordia Media Award and was voted the best journalist on campus by his fellow students. From his experience as editor in chief of *The Link*, Concordia's student paper, he went on to freelance for publications including Toronto's *Now* magazine, the *Montreal Mirror*, *Tart* and the *Globe and Mail Online Edition*. René also spent two years as a walking tour guide in southern Ontario. He is fascinated by the way places affect people's lives and plans to study urban planning at Ryerson University.